FLATHEAD FEVER
HOW TO HOT ROD THE FAMOUS FORD FLATHEAD V8

By Mike Davidson

First published in 1995 by
Graffiti Publications Pty. Ltd.,
69 Forest street, Castlemaine, Victoria, Australia.
Phone International 61 54 72 3653
or Fax 61 54 72 3805

Copyright 1995 by Mike Davidson.

First edition ISBN 0 949398 96 9

Second edition published in 1996 by
Graffiti Publications Pty. Ltd.,
69 Forest street, Castlemaine, Victoria, Australia.
Phone International 61 54 72 3653
or Fax 61 54 72 3805

Copyright 1996 by Mike Davidson.

Printed and bound in Australia.

ISBN 0 949398 25 X

ACKNOWLEDGEMENTS

I would like to thank several people for their assistance:-
    Chris Milton Engine Developments (Use of flow bench and machining)
    West Torrens Dyno Centre (Chassis dyno)
    Len Vodic (Graphics)
    Garth Butterworth (Engine assembly)
Every effort has been made to supply accurate information but no guarantee is
implied or given that the results achieved in this book can be duplicated.

                                                                    Mike Davidson

INTRODUCTION

The Ford Sidevalve V8 or as it is most commonly known "Flathead" has been with us since 1932 and has been a favourite with hot rodders since that time. The Flathead is currently experiencing a resurgence in popularity as older hot rodders rediscover the magic and younger ones discover it for the first time.

With the availability of more modern technology new speed equipment is now available to enable these engines to produce horsepower far in excess of their makers' wildest dreams.

This book covers the buildup of two such engines, one is coupled to a two speed Powerglide auto and fitted in a '22T Ford Roadster used as everyday transport and run at nostalgia drags, while the other is a pure race engine, coupled to a Saginaw four speed and fitted in a '27T Ford Roadster used on the salt flats.

The street engine as described in this book is the powerplant for the author's 1922 Ford Model T street rod which will also see occasional duty at the street rod drags. Overall the roadster is a real nostalgia piece but the transmission has been updated to a Powerglide.

Enough to make any Flathead fan drool with excitement! The entire engine and transmission package is painted bright red while the exhaust headers are silver. It's hard to imagine how you could make a Flathead look more attractive.

The race engine powers Mike Davidson's salt lake racer which is based on a '27 T Ford roadster. One glance at this Flathead tells you it means business. There has been no compromise in the search of ultimate Flathead horsepower!

FLATHEAD FEVER
How to Hot Rod the Famous Ford Flathead V8

BLOCKS

Right from their introduction in 1932 the Flathead Ford V8 has been a hit with hot rodders. The engine was made in a number of sizes and configurations over the years of production but for per-formance applications only two versions are worthy of serious consideration. Essentially these are the early and late 24 stud head models initially introduced in 1939 and updated in 1949. The earlier 21

The difference between the two 24 stud blocks is obvious. The block in the foreground is the later 8BA while at the rear is the early version with its half bellhousing. Note the difference in water passages. In the early blocks, water enters the front travelling to the rear, moving upwards it enters the head, finally exiting in the centre of the head. On the late block the water passages are larger at the rear allowing more flow in this area and finally exiting in the front of the head. If you wish to fit late heads on an early block these rear water passages must be enlarged to match the heads. The two most forward water passages in the heads must be filled as they do not match the block and conversely if fitting early heads to a late block the two water passages in the block must be filled.

stud engines were the hot set up in their day but really can't match the 24 stud models for performance potential. This book deals only with the 24 stud engines.

The 24 stud block was introduced in 1939 with 3-1/16" bore, 221 cubic inches and producing 85 HP. It was used in Ford passenger cars and commercial vehicles. The 3-3/16" bore, 239 cubic inch, 95 HP version was used in Mercury passenger cars and trucks until after the war when the horsepower was increased to 90 and 100 respectively. About this time the valves were moved .090" further up in the block and these blocks can be identified by oblong water holes above the valves.

In 1949 the water passages were changed necessitating the use of individual cylinder heads where previously they were interchangeable. The 1/2 bellhousing was removed from the rear of the block and replaced with a bolt-on pressed steel unit and later cast iron. Horsepower remained at 100 but on the Mercury the stroke was increased from 3-3/4" to 4" giving 255 cubic inches and 110 horsepower, Eventually horsepower was increased to 125 HP.

Many theories abound over which is the best block to use in a modified application, but as the ready source for these engines dries up, any 24 stud block that is in good useable condition should be considered. I personally went through ten blocks to find the two used in this book.

To determine whether a block is suitable, check the area between the valve seat and the edge of the bore on the intake and exhaust and between the centre main bearing and cam bearing web. If they are cracked you will be able to see the cracks with the naked eye. Once the block has been completely stripped I like to poke and prod with a large screwdriver to loosen up any obvious rust and scale that can be seen. I then lift the block on to the intake face and rock it onto the deck and then back to the intake and on to the other side deck for a few minutes, sweeping away the rubbish regularly with a small broom.

Next it's off to the machine shop to have the block hot tanked. Most machine shops tank blocks for about 12 hours, but for one of these engines it is not nearly long enough. I like to tank them for about two days, remove and wash down with high pressure water and re-tank for another two days. This might seem like overkill, but you would be amazed at the amount of rust and scale that builds up in a block over a period of 50 years. Remember that the cleaner the block is, the cooler the engine will run.

The next step whilst at the machine shop is to have the block magnafluxed (crack tested) as there might be a problem that cannot be seen. Follow this with sonic checking to determine the thickness of the bores. Most blocks will safely bore 1/8", but having it checked is good insurance.

Now that the block has checked out OK and is thoroughly clean, it should be closely inspected for casting flash that may break off and find its way into the oil pump. Remove with a small die grinder fitted with a small drum sander. I then paint all internal surfaces with red oxide enamel using a 1/2" wide brush. This will seal off the pores of the cast iron and assist with oil return, and if the block is sitting for any length of time will prevent rust from forming on the exposed surfaces.

To determine what block you have check the codes below: (Canada and Australia – Sample only). These codes are stamped on the intake face of the block.

C Represents Canadian design.

O Represents the model year for which part was designed; 8=1938, 9=1939, 0=1940, 1=1941, 2=1942, 3=1943, 4=1944, etc.

I Represents the engine type;
   1=85 HP V-8, 2=60 HP V-8, 9=95 HP V-8.

6 Represents the vehicle wheel base;
   1=101" WB, 8=158" WB, 6=176" WB 4=94" WB

T Specifies the type of vehicle;
   A – Passenger, B – Bus, C – Commercial, D – 3/4 Ton, T – Regular Truck, U – Dump, V – Drop Frame, W – Cab-Over-Engine, Y – 1 Ton.

F Designates right-hand drive.

Arrow indicates the location of the engine identification number on Australian and Canadian sourced blocks.

U.S. manufactured flatheads have a variety of identification numbers and codes which are shown in the table on the next page.

FIRST SERIAL AND ENGINE NUMBERS

FORD V8 1935-53

Year	Model	Number
1935	48	18-123457
1936	68	18-2207111
1937	74	54-6602
	78	18-3331857
1938	82A	54-358335
	81A	18-4186447
1939	922A	Continued from 1938
	91A	18-4661001
1940	022A	54-506501
	01A	18-5210701
1941	11A	18-5896295
1942	21A	18-6769036
1946	69A	99A-650280
1947	79A	799A-1412708
1948	89A	899A-1984859
1949	8BA	8BA-101
1950	0BA	B0-100001*
1951	1BA	B1-100001*
1952	B2	B2-100001*
1953	B3	B3-100001*

MERCURY V8 1939-53

Year	Model	Number
1939	99A	99A-1
1940	09A	99A-101701
1941	19A	99A-257101
1942	29A	99A-466701
1946	69M	99A-650280
1947	79M	799A-1412708
1948	89M	899A-200502028
1949	9CM	9CM-101
1950	0CM	50-10001M*
1951	1CM	51-10001M*
1952	All	52-10001M*
1953	All	53-10001M*

Location – 1935-48: On top of clutch housing and on left frame near cowl.

1949-53: Plate on dash.

*Additional letters between basic model letters and serial numbers denote assembly plant.

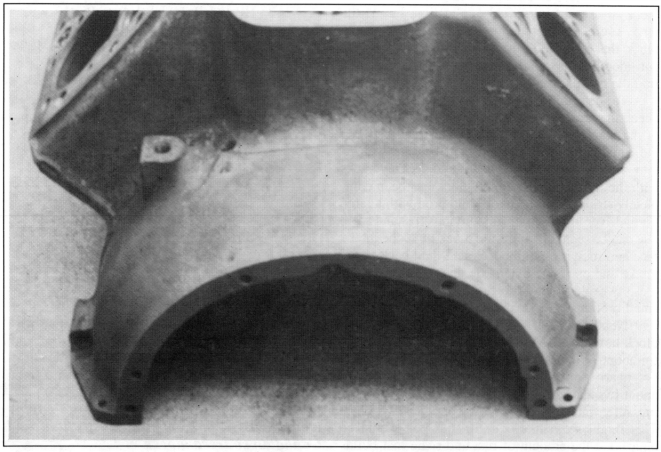

Easiest way to recognise an "early" 24 stud Flathead block is to check the bellhousing area at the rear of the block. These blocks have part of the bellhousing cast with the block as shown in the photo above. Check the comparison photos on the next page to see the difference on a "late" block.

Here is a bird's eye view of the rear of both blocks. The early block contains the rear main seal within the bearing cap while the 8BA has the lower half of the seal in the pan.

STREET ROD BLOCK
STD BORE

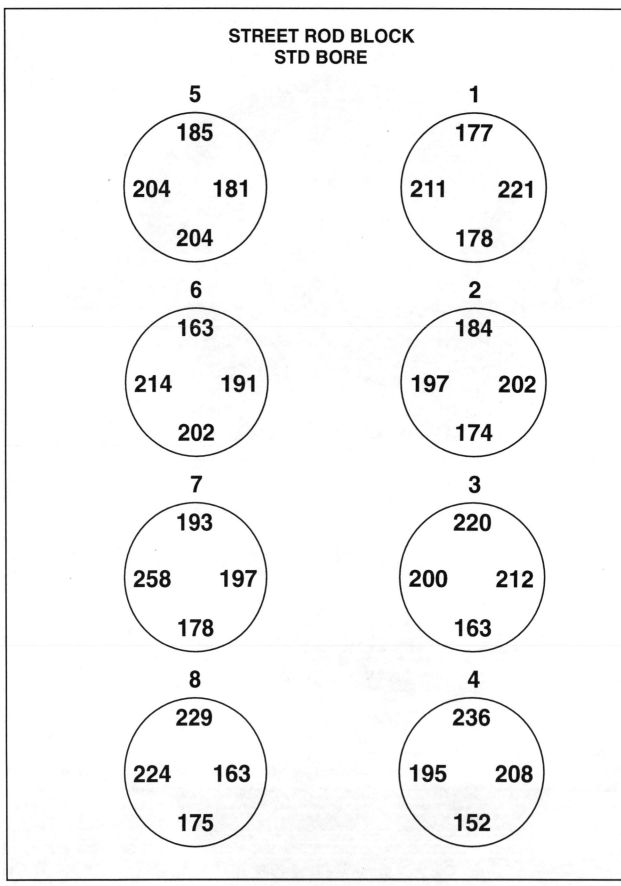

5

185
204   181
204

1

177
211   221
178

6

163
214   191
202

2

184
197   202
174

7

193
258   197
178

3

220
200   212
163

8

229
224   163
175

4

236
195   208
152

I have sonic checked several blocks over the years – this is a fair representation of how thick they are. Boring the blocks to 3-5/16" will remove approximately .060" each side of the cylinder, leaving enough material for another rebore at a later date should this become necessary.

RACE BLOCK
STD BORE

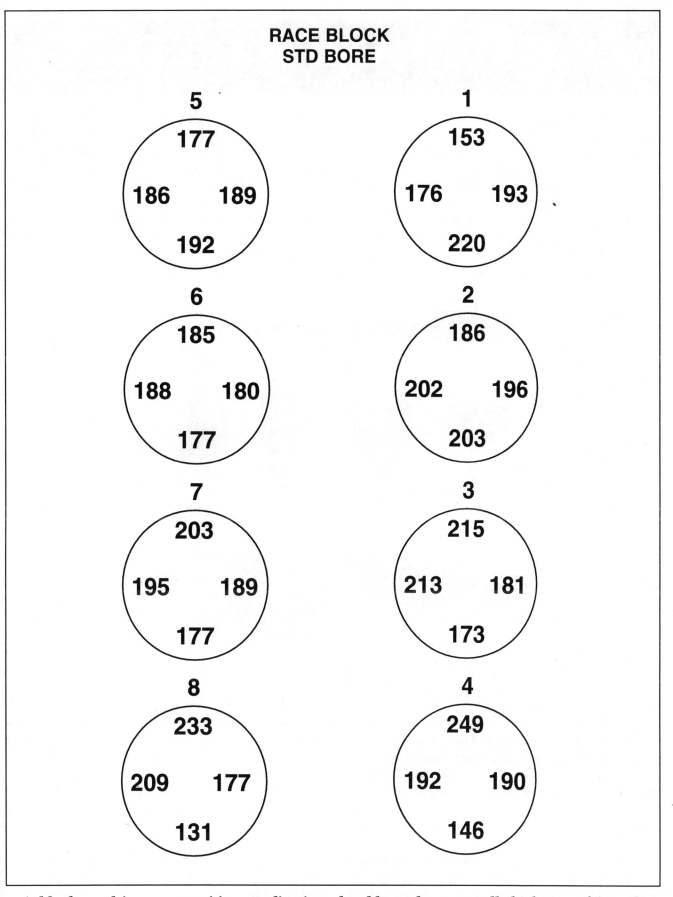

A block used in a competition application should not have a wall thickness of less than 0.100" on the thrust side (the left hand side of the cylinders looking from the front) as bore flexing will occur. If sonic checking a block that has been fitted with sleeves only the thickness of the sleeve will be recorded.

PORTING AND RELIEVING

The biggest single factor that effects the potential of an engine is the ability to breathe (and these engines need all the help they can get). If it will not breathe it will not produce horsepower.

Flow benches have been around for a number of years, but were few and far between when hot rodders first started modifying the Flathead. Now they are more accessible and a necessary tool in the quest for maximum efficiency.

cylinder a three angle valve job, installed standard Ford valves and guides with checking springs. Next I installed a Kong Jackson cylinder head (used in all flows) with a .030" thick solid aluminium head gasket and fitted it on a Superflow 600 flow bench. I fitted a depth gauge to the lifter bores to measure the valve lift in increments of .075" to .450" (the lift of the cam to be used) and measured all flows at 10 inches of water.

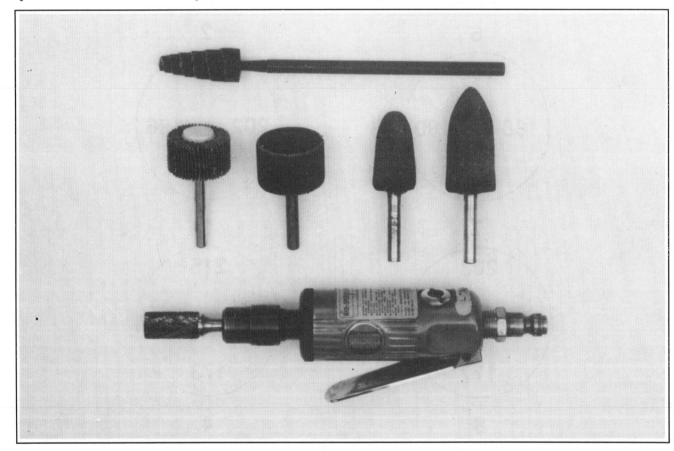

I prefer to use an air operated die grinder and this one is about as small as they come, allowing easy access to the hard to get at areas. The cross cut burr fitted to the grinder makes short work of the excess material that needs to be removed followed by the mounted points to remove any ripples and bumps. Following this the drum sander will leave a smooth consistent finish while in the hard to get at areas I use the poli-roll on the extension. Last of all is the 60 grit polishing fan which will remove any small imperfections leaving a smooth matt finish.

To best understand how the ports work I cut up a discarded block for a closer inspection. The casting is approximately 3/16" thick, so trying to make some significant improvement without grinding away any more material than necessary is not easy. I bored one bank of cylinders out to 3-5/16", the bore size both engines will be, and gave No. 1

Intake Lift	.075	.150	.225	.300	.375	.450
CFM	20.2	34.4	45.1	48.1	49.3	51.1
Exhaust Lift						
CFM	20.8	35.6	43.4	47.5	49.2	49.9

As you can see the exhaust flowed 98 per cent of the intake in stock form, which shows how inef-

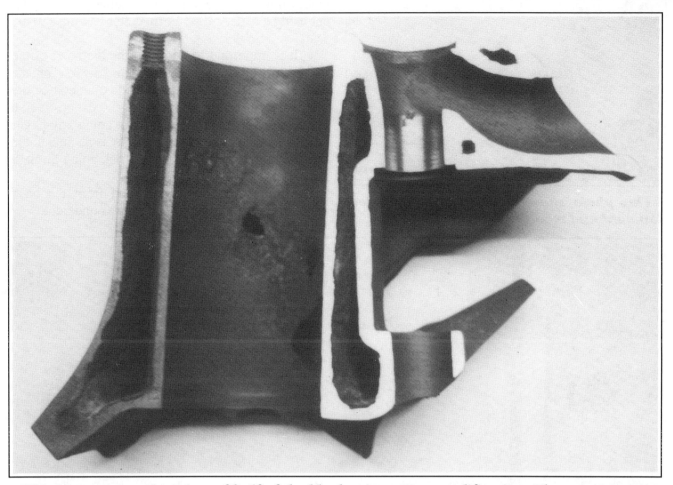

This is a cross section view of half of the block prior to any modification. The water passage above the short turn will vary in size from block to block and is the biggest single contributing factor which limits the amount of flow that can be achieved. Some engine builders have filled their blocks with aluminum, allowing them to port into the water passages greatly improving flow but this is not a practical alternative for a lot of applications. This block was originally destined for a 1939 truck and after many years of service was reconditioned (having a full set of cylinder sleeves fitted). It was installed in a speed boat used in salt water. After cutting it up and removing the sleeves the corrosion was obvious, having eaten through the cylinder walls to the sleeves in many places, and yet in the bottom right hand side of the block I still found foundry core sand – and they wonder why these engines run hot!

ficient the intake really is. Having a base line to work from I began modifying the ports as shown in the next table.

Ports cleaned up
     19.6 35   45.1 48.1 49.9 51.7
Deeper port – tapered guide
     20.2 33.8 46.3 49.9 51.7 53.5
Radius valve seat – radius guide
     22.6 36.7 48.1 54   57   58.8

At this point the results show what can be achieved using standard components with only slight modification. All tests that follow show large increases in CFM as larger valves are used and the port shape is changed from an oval to a D.

1.625" valve – radius guide – radius seat
     24.8 44.5 56.4 63   68.3 71.3

These flows were made with OEM Chev valves modified in a lathe to reduce the back angle and radius on the underside of the head. At this point the tests show what is required to make any significant gains. A radiused valve guide flows slightly better than a tapered guide. A radiused valve seat flows better than a three angle and the more material that was removed from the back angle and radius of the valve the better it flows at higher lift.

To further improve on this using a 1.50" rose cutter the valve throat was enlarged to a depth of .500". A hardened valve insert 1.750" OD was fitted and a guide was radiused by hand with a file, center punched in several places to expand it so it

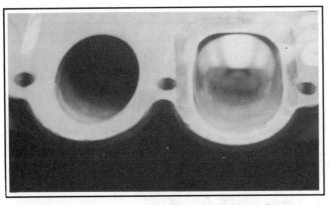

This photo shows a comparison between standard and modified ports.

would not move once it was installed and the seat cut using a MIRA 4043 Form cutter leaving a .040" seat.

It is important to note that the diameter of the valve throat should be between 86-88% of the diameter of the valve. The outside diameter of the inlet valve insert almost touches the exhaust valve insert, so I would recommend not going any larger on the intake, not only for this reason, but if the throat is enlarged any more you risk going through the casting.

More material was removed from the back angle of the valve, and the stem was undercut.

Shown here is one half of a block mounted on the flow bench with a Kong head installed. In the centre at the rear is a G clamp fitted to the centre exhaust port to stop the assembly moving while the tests are carried out. No. 2 port is being tested with valves and checking springs fitted while a depth gauge is fitted in the lifter bore to open the valve at intervals of .075". Over the entrance of the port is a venturi made from modelling clay to simulate actual operating conditions.

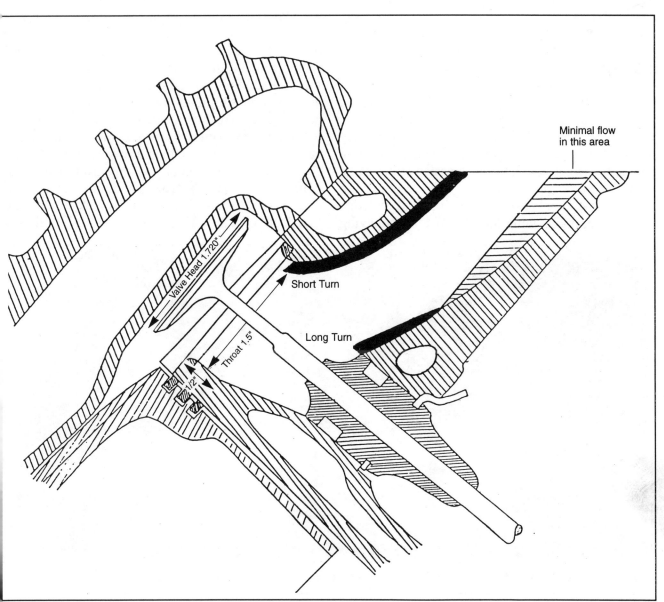

Minimal flow
in this area

Valve Head 1.720"

Short Turn

Long Turn

Throat 1.5"

As can be seen by the diagram only a small amount of material is removed from the long turn while the guide is scalloped rather than tapered as is traditionally the case (worth 1 extra CFM), while most of the material is removed from the short turn.

25   43   57   68.5 76   80.7

Prior to this I had put in a special order to Manley for eight 1.72" stainless steel one piece race flow valves to suit a S/B Chev. These are a smaller version of their 2.02 valve, and were only marginally more expensive, and much easier than turning down the larger ones on the lathe myself. After giving one a 30° back cut (worth one additional c.f.m.) I tried again but no significant change from the previous flow was evident. I then modified the cylinder head altering the shape of the casting between the valve and piston and made another flow.

25.1 43.8 58.1 70   79   85

I then turned my attention to the exhaust port, cleaning up the short turn and elongating the flange where the exhaust exits the block and fitted an off the shelf Manley 1.50" stainless steel one piece race

flow valve to suit a S/B Chev. The seat was cut using a MIRA 4005B form cutter leaving a .060" wide seat and giving the valve a 25° back cut.

22.3 42.4 53   57.9 61.5 62.9

The exhaust now flows 74% of the intake which is quite acceptable, with any significant improvement over this requiring major surgery on the block. Because I am using Offenhauser cylinder heads on my street engine I thought it would be interesting to do a couple of comparison flows. 1.720" OEM valve.

23.2 38.5 53   68.5 78.2 81.2

1.720" Manley race flow valve

24.4 40.7 56.5 70.7 79.7 85.6

As you can see there is almost no difference in flow between the two cylinder heads, but there are other things to be considered which are covered in a later chapter.

Using the formula :-

85(CFM) x .43 = 36.55 x 8 (No. of cylinders) = 292.4 HP is possible – on paper at least.

I have conducted approximately 40 flows and the results shown here are a selection to give an idea of what can be achieved step by step.

There are mixed theories about relieving blocks. Compression is lost, but I would prefer an engine to have a little less compression and breathe well. Several engine builders of late are preferring to radius the area between the valves and the edge of the bore, maintaining the deck height, believing the material removed in the traditional relief will not unduly effect flow and may make the top edge of the bore more susceptible to cracking. I simulated this relief with modelling clay and lost 12 c.f.m. I have also seen many standard blocks crack in this area so I doubt if the removal of any material in this area would make any difference. In the years I have worked on these engines the one block that is more susceptible to cracking than any other is the C59A.

To relieve the block without losing too much compression make a template of the combustion chamber and transfer it onto the block, machining to a depth of .125". This can be done on a mill, or a

This is what the relief looks like on the street block prior to assembly.

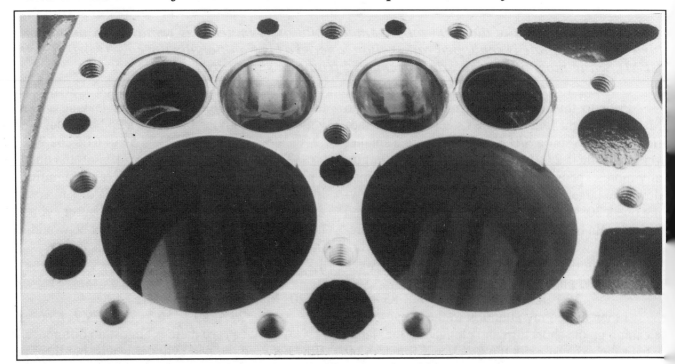

This is what the relief looks like on the race block prior to assembly.

cheaper alternative is a router using a burr or mounted point. The sharp edge left after machining at the top of the bore should then be radiused. The block for my street engine is factory relieved and although not ideal I have left it as is. After decking it is .100"deep. The block for my race car was set up in a mill to maintain accuracy, and milled to a depth of .110" and after decking is .100" deep. I have been conservative here as the Kong heads have quite large combustion chambers, and I do not want to lose too much compression.

Other types of heads may require a different relief shape in the block. A typical example is Offenhauser heads which work best with a more curved relief as shown in the accompanying photo.

Right: Offenhauser heads require a different shaped relief to that used for the Kong heads. In the Offy case the relief is a more curved shape.

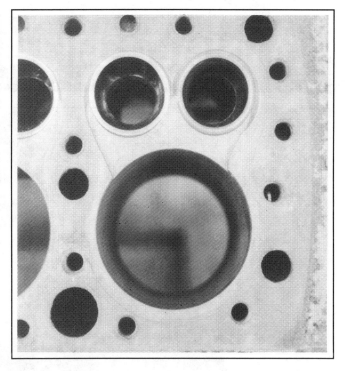

CAMSHAFT – LIFTERS – VALVE SPRINGS

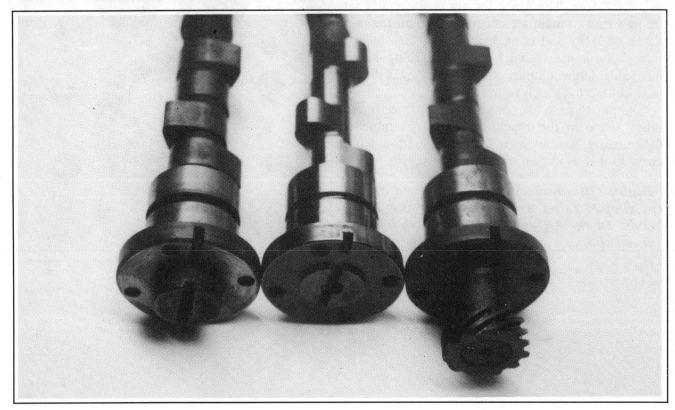

The cam on the left is an original, the type used with a diver's helmet distributor up until 1942. In the centre is the billet roller cam with the shorter nose which used the crab distributor from 1942-1948 while on the right is an 8BA cam reground by Isky.

Choosing the right cam depends on a variety of considerations including engine displacement, transmission, differential ratio, weight of the vehicle and its intended use.

In the case of my street engine, at 276 cu. in. using a manually shifted auto transmission with high stall converter, a rough idle will not be a problem. Rear end ratio of 3.45:1 and an all up weight of approximately 1800lb. I prefer a cam with a lot of lift to enhance breathing with moderate duration for drivability and have selected an Isky 400 Jr. with .400" lift 258° duration and a set of hollow Johnson adjustable lifters, Isky dual valve springs and retainers.

The cam required for my race car engine will need to be a lot more radical. Given the application of this vehicle a cam with as much lift and duration as a I can obtain should work well. A very rough idle and poor low end torque will not be a problem as I am looking for top end performance only, and at 284 cu. in. with a four speed, quick change rear end and an all up weight of approximately 2,000lb, I have selected a Crower billet roller cam with

.458" lift 290° duration, Crower roller lifters, Crane dual valve springs and retainers. When selecting a cam for a supercharged engine it should have an advertised duration of between 280° - 290°.

A problem faced when fitting a modified camshaft in a Flathead, be it a reground original or a new billet, is the smaller base circle, which allows the lifter to fit further down the lifter bore leaving additional clearance between the lifter and valve. Fitting adjustable lifters should cure this problem, but unfortunately the adjusting bolts are screwed into the lifter too far in the factory, and if using a camshaft with any lift greater than approximately .330" the bolts will have to be screwed out. This loosens the tension on the interference thread. At this point the only quick fix is to put Loctite on the threads and hope for the best. I should mention also that the factory does not supply the adjusting bolts as a spare part.

Another problem encountered when adjusting the bolts is the interference between the open end wrench and the top of the lifter bore resulting in small deposits of cast iron filings in the valley. To

Here is a selection of types of lifters used in the majority of applications. On the left is a new Johnson (solid) adjustable lifter while next to it is the older Johnson (hollow), now no longer available, but still very desirable because of its light weight. The two on the right are original Ford, the first being an 8BA which used parallel stem valves while the other is from an early engine which used mushroom stem valves. Parallel stem valves should never be fitted with lifters from an early engine as the possibility exists for the valve to punch a hole through the top of the lifter.

A lifter seldom seen these days in a flathead is the mushroom, used because of its larger base giving more lobe contact with the cam and therefore more duration. The lifter in the centre is an original Ford fitted with a contact pad which was faced to give the correct valve clearance. A slot running its full length on one side accommodates a wire staple that was attached to the lifter bore to stop it from turning, while the base was radius ground to give a roller effect. On the right is a new adjustable roller which has two small needle rollers protruding from one side that fit into a slot in the lifter bore to stop it from rotating. While the obvious advantages of a roller setup are less friction giving less wear and more horsepower, the ramps on a roller cam lobe are actually concave and only a roller lifter will follow this profile.

Here the jig can be seen fitted to the lifter bore prior to drilling for the roller lifter.

overcome these problems I am using S/B Chev valves which are approximately .060" longer than Ford valves, therefore allowing the bolts to be screwed further into the lifters making for a tighter fit. A plunge cut is made on the top of each lifter bore to a depth of .100" leaving additional clearance between the top of the lifter bore and the adjusting bolt.

To stop the lifter from turning while adjusting it, LH and RH wrenches are available which clip onto the adjacent valve for support, but they are cumbersome. The easiest and quickest method is to drill a 3/16" hole two thirds of the way down the lifter bore and insert a 5/32" pin punch, locating it in one of the slots in the side of the lifter.

The lifter bore facing tool is shown and the amount of material removed can easily be seen from the adjacent lifter bores. Also shown are the 3/16" holes drilled to stop the lifter from turning while it is being adjusted. After the lifter bores have been faced and drilled a fine grit 1" diameter ball hone is used to remove any sharp edges and leave a smooth finish.

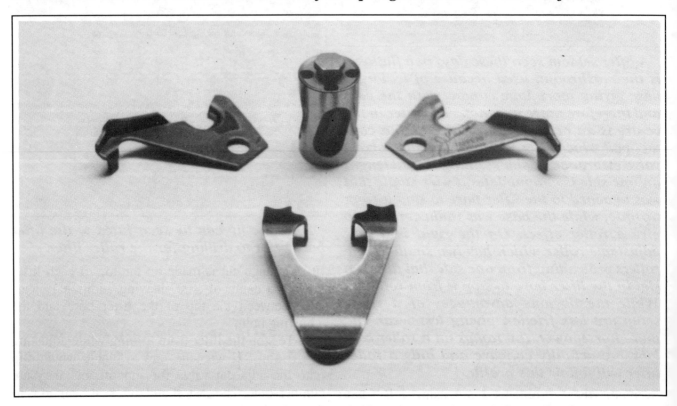

On either side of the lifter are the left and right hand wrenches while at the front is one of a different design. These are a must if fitting adjustable lifters to an engine in operating condition where it is impractical to drill the lifter bores.

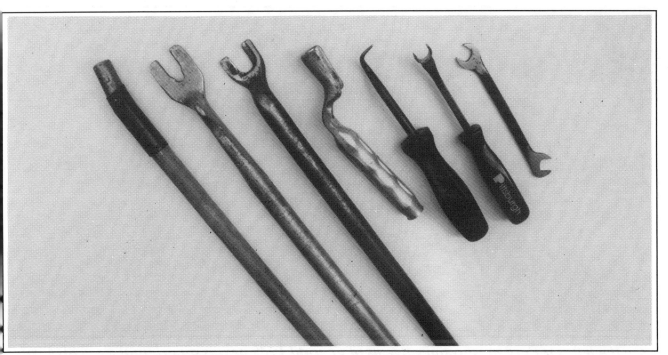

A selection of the tools required to remove and install the valve train. From the right is a 7/16" open end wrench for adjusting the lifters, an owner made tool for holding the valve collets in place while assembling dual valve springs, a pick for removing the guide retaining clip, a drift for loosening stubborn valve guides prior to removing the retaining clip, two styles of valve guide remove/install bars, one of Ford (military) design and one made by the author, and an owner made guide removing drift.

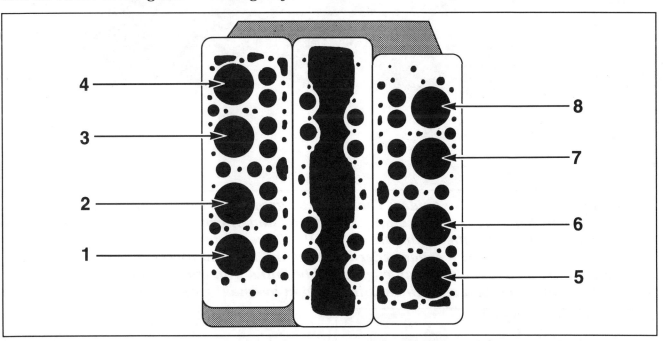

To adjust the valve clearances we must first check the firing order which is

| 1 5 4 8 |
| 6 3 7 2 |

Having written these down like this makes it easier to follow when making the adjustments. *Rotate the crank until No. 1 cylinder is rocking and adjust the clearance on No. 6, continuing with No. 5 rocking adjust No. 3, No. 4 rocking adjust No. 7, No. 8 rocking adjust No. 2. Now reverse the procedure No. 6 rocking adjust No. 1. No. 3 rocking adjust No. 5, No. 7 rocking adjust No. 4, No. 2 rocking adjust No. 8.*

It should be noted that the cylinders are numbered from the front on the left hand side (looking front to rear) 1 2 3 4 and on the right hand side 5 6 7 8. Number one is not the most forward cylinder which is opposite to normal procedure with most U.S. designed V8 engines.

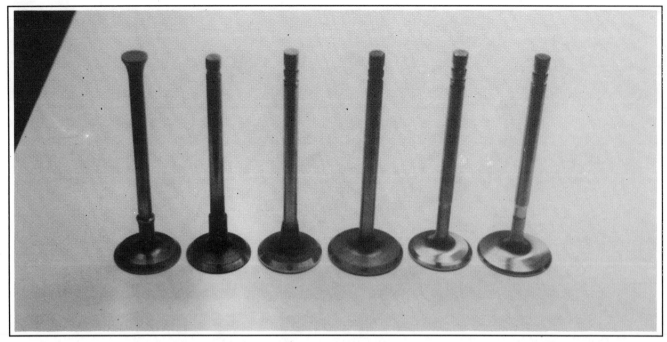

On the left is a Ford mushroom valve used up until 1949 next is an original Ford 8BA valve followed by OEM SB Chev exhaust, intake, race flow SB Chev exhaust and intake.

There are two types of valve guides. The split type used in all early engines in conjunction with mushroom stem valves with a diameter of 5/16" and one piece used in all 8BA engines with parallel stem valves with a diameter of 11/32". There are two variations of the one-piece guide, an intake defined by a square edged slot around its circumference to take a seal and the exhaust which does not. Often an engine will be found with only one or the other, but can easily be modified to take a seal which is included in overhaul gasket sets.

Isky single valve spring part number 185g with 1949–51 Ford retainer and collets. A 0.140" thick shim is also used in this application because the Isky spring is shorter than the original Ford spring.

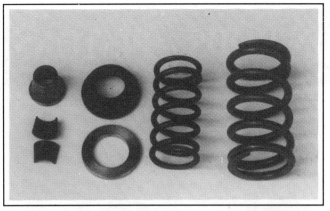

Isky dual valve springs part number 4005 with the retainer part number 87F, shim part number 85F, 1952–54 Ford retainer inserts and collets.

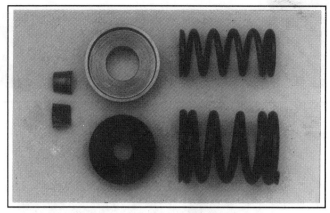

Crane dual valve springs part number 99834 (outer) 99858 (inner), retainers part number 99936 and machined collets. The shims are made from X4150 and are 0.400" thick.

VALVE ASSEMBLY

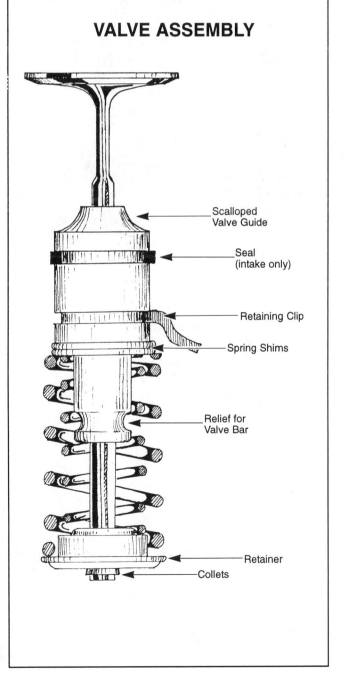

Scalloped Valve Guide

Seal (intake only)

Retaining Clip

Spring Shims

Relief for Valve Bar

Retainer

Collets

Chart showing valve spring pressure.

	Installed	Lift	
Standard Ford Valve	35lb	85lb	(.300)
Single Isky	45lb	125lb	(.300)
		140lb	(.350)
Dual Isky	75lb	175lb	(.400)
Dual Crane	140lb	330lb	(.460)

CRANKSHAFTS – CON RODS – PISTONS

On the left is a late 1930s crankshaft with two oil slingers at the rear which used a cup arrangement and not a wick seal to retain the oil. A single oil hole appears on each con rod journal which used the full floating style bearings. The second crankshaft was used from the mid 1940s and has a single oil slinger as did all crankshafts from the early 1940s on, but it has two oil holes per con rod journal and uses a very thick version of an insert bearing. The third crankshaft is essentially the same. Being from an 8BA the angle of the teeth on the timing gear are opposite to the early one and it has an oil seal retainer pressed onto the nose to retain the gear. On the early engines it was part of the bottom pulley. The fourth crankshaft is a four inch Mercury and other than the larger stroke is the same as the previous one.

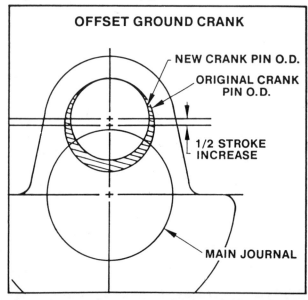

OFFSET GROUND CRANK

NEW CRANK PIN O.D.

ORIGINAL CRANK PIN O.D.

1/2 STROKE INCREASE

MAIN JOURNAL

If wanting to increase the displacement of an engine, stroking is the most efficient way. All cranks used in these engines have 3-3/4" stroke with the exception of the '49-'53 Mercury which has a stroke of 4". All have 2.498" main and 2.138" conrod journals with the exception of the 221 cu in engine which has 1.998" conrod journals. By offset grinding the con rod journals .0625" to 1.998", 1/8" extra stroke can be achieved. All cranks are made of nodular iron (cast) with the exception of a small percentage of '49-'53 Mercurys that were forged steel.

For the street engine I am using a 4" Mercury crank and con rods. These con rods differ from their Ford counterpart as they have oil bleed holes drilled

A closer look at the two later crankshafts will determine which one is the Mercury. The 5/8" core plug in the end of the conrod journal gives it away.

I have seen one Mercury crankshaft that didn't have the telltale 5/8" core plug, so the other way to check is to measure the width of the counterweights, the difference is approximately 1/2" with the Mercury being wider.

in them and they have been magnafluxed, polished, shot peened, resized, rebushed and fitted with new S/B Chev con rod nuts. Fitted to these I am using locally made JP cast pistons made from LM13 high silicone aluminum. (More than 12% silicone makes them a hypereutectic piston). These pistons are also available from Motor City Flathead.

For the race car engine a 4" Mercury crank is being used that has been stroked to 4-1/8" and due to the lighter than stock all up weight of the pistons and con rods the crank counterweights were turned down in a lathe to keep the recirculating mass as

light as possible without affecting the balance. The crank has also been tufftrided, which is a process where the crank is heated to 800°F and dumped in a bath of cyanide salt to harden the outer .015" of the shaft prior to being finish ground. When ground it will have a .010" hardened skin on the bearing surfaces to prevent wear.

Although Ford con rods will take a lot of punishment (due to good quality steel and their length) I have reservations in using them for this application. Instead I have opted for a set of Howards forged aluminum con rods but due to the length of forgings available these con rods are 6-5/8" C/C instead of the usual Ford 7" C/C. They are fitted with Arias forged pistons.

After the crankshaft has been ground the oil holes should be chamfered eliminating the possibility if any sharp edges being picked up by the bearings, and providing a small reservoir to help distribute the oil.

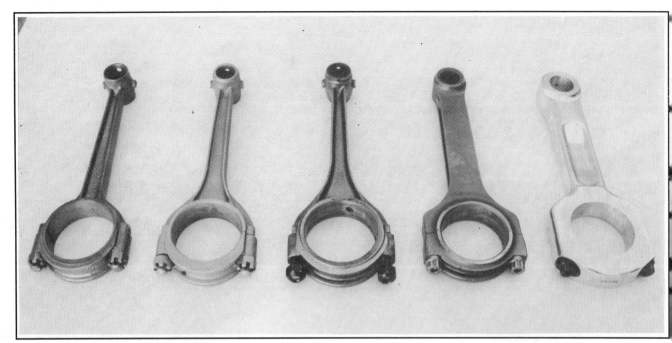

On the left is a con rod from a 21 stud engine that is often used when building a stroked engine. The con rod next to it is a 21A found in 3-1/16'' bore 24 stud engines and being marginally stronger is more popular in a stroked application. The third con rod is from a Mercury and is essentially the same as any other 8BA con rod, but does have an oil bleed hole to direct excess oil towards the camshaft. If intending to use original con rods, measure the length of each one, fitting the longer ones to the LHS of the engine as this side has slightly less compression due to the different inclination of the valves from one side to the other. The Mercury con rods I am using in my street engine all measured within .010''. The fourth con rod is a Cunningham billet (Carrillo style) and although a little heavy at 668 grams as compared to the Mercury at 523 grams is the ultimate for strength and durability. The fifth con rod is a Howard aluminum billet weighing a mere 503 grams but a con rod of this nature has a limited life span.

With the 3/8'' over standard stroke and the chunky aluminum con rods, the bottom of each cylinder had to be relieved as well as around one core plug boss for clearance.

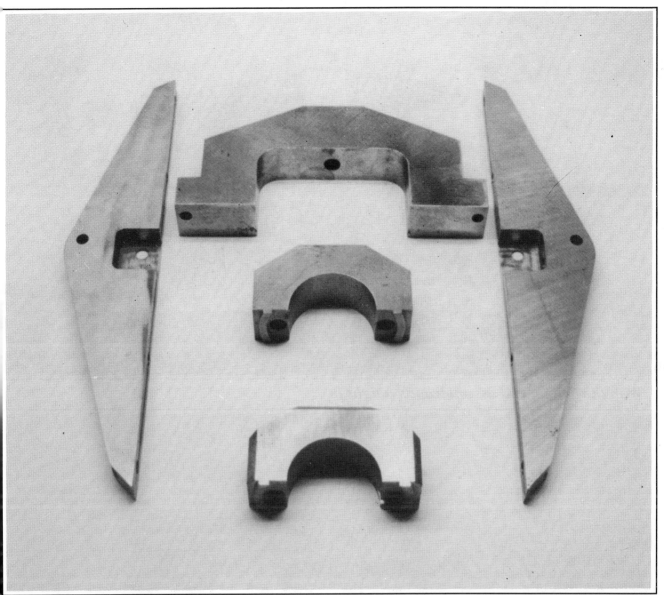

To hold the bottom end together in a performance application steel bearing caps on the front and center main are essential. A steel girdle is also mandatory for a race engine. Bearing clearances are critical on any engine and even more so in a performance application. In the street engine I am using Federal Mogul 533M main bearings with a clearance of (.0025") torqued to 90 ft lbs while for the con rods Federal Mogul 1505CAA with a clearance of (.0025") torqued to 50 ft lbs with side clearances of (.012"). In the race engine I am again using Federal Mogul 533M main bearings with a clearance of .0025" on each end with .003" in the center torquing the front and center cap to 105 ft lb and the rear to 90 ft lb while the girdle is torqued 45 ft lb all round. For the con rod bearings I am using narrowed and pinned Clevite 77 CB610P with a clearance of .0032" torqued to 70 ft lb with side clearance of .025".

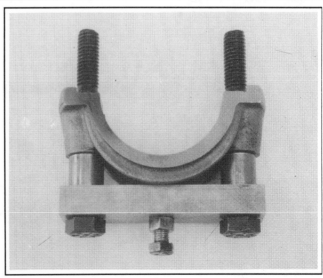

A cheaper alternative to a steel bearing cap is a main bearing support. These are usually fitted to the center bearing cap and due to extra clearance can be fitted to the front cap in an 8BA engine as well.

With the bottom end assembled it's a tight fit.

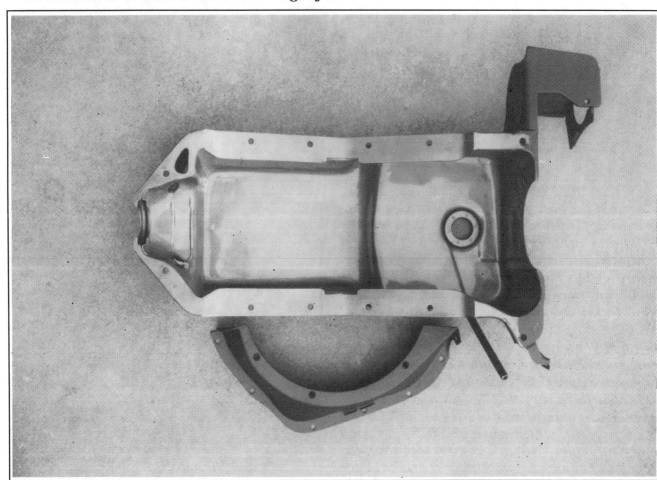

Fitting the bottom end together is one thing, making the pan fit is another. The front of the pan needed a lot of reworking with a hammer and a torch, while the sides were trimmed and new rails were made from 1-1/2" x 1/8" flat. Notice that this is a truck pan with a removable rear section making access to the clutch possible without dropping the pan.

The piston on the left is an original Ford with ring widths of 3/32"– 3/32"– 3/16"– 3/16" which feature a split skirt design allowing a much tighter fit of .001"– 0015" for quiet running with a top radius of 7-1/8". Next is the JP using an identical pin to the Ford with ring widths of 5/64"– 5/64"– 5/32", a chrome top and plain second ring with a tolerance of .003" and weighing 412 grams with a top radius of 5-3/8". On the right is the Arias forged piston using a .920" diameter tapered pin retained with single spirolox and ring widths of 1/16"– 5/64"– 5/32" with a ductile chrome top and total seal second ring. These weigh 379 grams and have a top radius of 4-1/16". Due to the hard, smooth surface of chrome faced compression rings a relatively coarse 280 grit stone is used to hone the bores.

To make piston installation easier in a relieved block, I made a sleeve from scrap pipe tapered on the inside to the diameter of the bore and trimmed to fit into the relief, eliminating the possibility of rings popping out.

OIL PUMPS – FILTERS

On the left is the standard oil pump found in engines up to the early 1940s followed by a revised version which had longer gears and a relief valve fitted to its stem to override the one in the front of the valley. The third pump is found in all 8BA engines and is the recommended one to use in all applications. Last but not least is the big brother to the 8BA pump unfortunately no longer available, this one will be fitted to my race engine.

Of the several oil pumps used in these engines, the later 8BA is the only one to use, eclipsed only by the aftermarket high volume pumps available in the '50s. The timing gears in early blocks are lubricated when the oil pump relief valve lifts off its seat during engine warm up and through windage. This works fine on standard and mild performance engines, but on the race engine with high valve spring pressure creating additional load on the timing gears, additional lubrication is required. I have removed the relief valve and spring, tapped the drain hole 1/4" UNC and fitted a button head bolt with a .030" hole drilled through it to provide constant lubrication without affecting oil pressure.

The oil filters fitted to these engines are a bypass type and although they can be made to look very attractive by swapping for the re-released beehive canister it would be my last choice of the three available options. The most efficient way to filter the oil is to plumb the oil directly from the bottom of the pump out of the pan into the filter and back into the main oil gallery. There is a kit available for this conversion using an 8BA pump, but the easiest method which works with all pumps is to run a 1/2" UNF tap all the way into the the horizontal oil gallery (where the takeoff for the bypass unit connects) and then plug with a grub screw of the same size. As the oil leaves the pump a small percentage lubricates the rear main bearing, and the rest is then directed out of the block to the filter, and back to the main oil gallery.

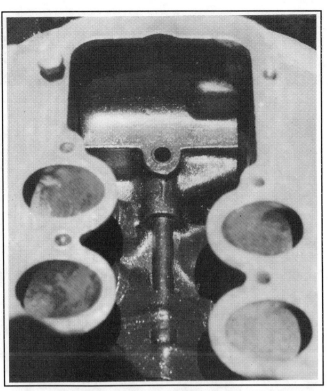

Unless using the original fuel pump in an early engine the pushrod sleeve should be removed, tapped 1/2" UNC and a bolt and flat washer fitted to eliminate excess oil splash and loss of pressure.

On 8BA blocks the modification detailed in fig. 29 is unnecessary as the main oil gallery bypasses this area, however, I would recommend drilling a .030" hole in the main oil gallery plug located in the front of the the block to supply additional lubrication to this area.

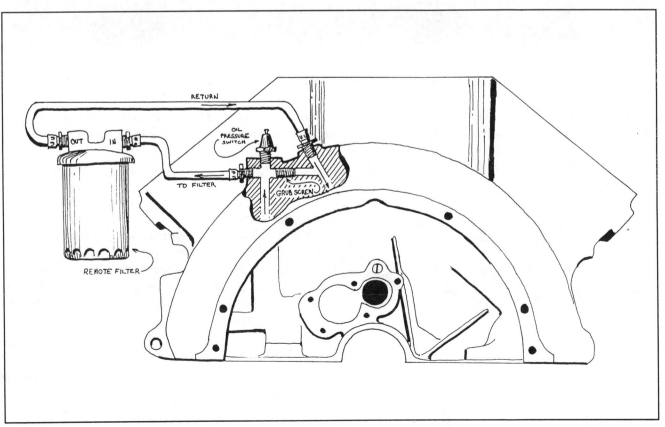

Oil filter diagram.

CYLINDER HEADS

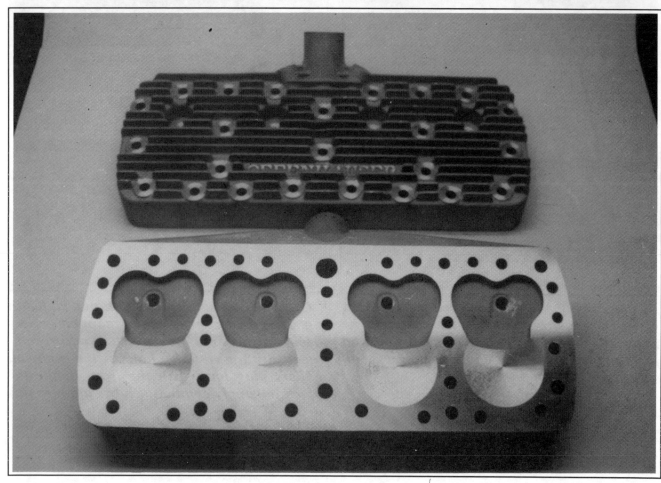

The Offenhauser cylinder head, although more robust in construction with larger cooling capacity is not a lot different from the original Ford aluminum cylinder head. They are available in a variety of compression ratios which is stamped near the water outlet. These are marked .425" which refers to the depth of the combustion chamber around the top edge of the valve pocket and measure 62.39cc (see attached compression ratio chart 32A).

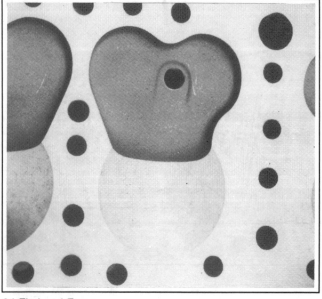

In the quest for high compression some engine builders will use a head with a shallow combustion chamber and machine additional clearance around the valves, only to create another problem. The area between the valve pocket and piston relief is where most of the flow is obtained and must also be relieved, lowering the compression. By using .425" heads good flow will be achieved without having to make any modifications, and if looking for more compression, fitting pop-up pistons is the way to go.

COMPRESSION RATIO CHART

| Engine Size | | Head Numbers | | | | | Cubic Inch |
Bore	Stroke	No. 425	No. 400	No. 375	No. 350	No. 325	Displacement
3-1/16	3-3/4	7.1	7.6	7.9	8.5	9.2	220.92
3-1/16	3-7/8	7.2	7.7	8.2	8.8	9.5	228.28
3-1/16	4	7.4	7.9	8.4	9.0	9.8	235.648
3-3/16	3-3/4	7.4	7.9	8.5	9.2	9.9	239.312
3-3/16	3-7/8	7.7	8.2	8.8	9.4	10.2	247.288
3-3/16	4	8.0	8.5	9.0	9.7	10.5	255.272
3-3/16	4-1/8	8.2	8.7	9.3	9.9	10.8	263.24
3-5/16	3-3/4	8.1	8.6	9.1	9.8	10.6	258.48
3-5/16	3-7/8	8.3	8.8	9.4	10.1	10.9	267.096
3-5/16	4	8.6	9.1	9.7	10.4	11.3	275.712
3-5/16	4-1/8	8.8	9.3	9.9	10.7	11.6	284.328
3-3/8	3-3/4	8.3	8.8	9.4	10.1	10.9	268.376
3-3/8	3-7/8	8.6	9.1	9.7	10.4	11.3	277.328
3-3/8	4	8.9	9.4	10.0	10.7	11.6	286.272
3-3/8	4-1/8	9.1	9.6	10.3	11.1	11.9	295.20

| V8-60 Engine | | Head Numbers | | | Cubic Inch |
Bore	Stroke	No. 300	No. 275	No. 255	Displacement
2.600	3.200	9.5	10.5	11.5	135.912

Example: No. 400 indicates .400 valve clearance.
The above approximate compression ratios are figured on non-relieved blocks, ratio is lowered depending upon depth of relief. The compression ratios shown are only to be used as a guide and each engine should be checked individually.

Flathead engines suffer from lack of compression and high running temperature. Fitting aluminum cylinder heads goes a long way to solving these problems, but it is not all straight sailing.

Cylinder heads are still available from Edelbrock, Navarro, Offenhauser, Eddie Meyer and more recently Kong Jackson, Motor City Flathead and Tony Baron.

Very high compression is still difficult to achieve especially if using a cam with very high lift unless pop up pistons are used where the heads are fly cut to the diameter of the pistons to whatever depth is required to achieve the desired compression.

On the street engine I am using Offenhauser heads with a .425" valve clearance and a McCord 6082 head gasket with a crushed thickness of .050" giving .075" clearance. The clearance between the valve and head and piston and head should not be less than .060" as flow will suffer at high RPM and you risk having the pistons hit the head as the con rods do stretch. The Offenhauser heads are thicker than their Ford counterpart which enables them to hold more coolant, and being made of aluminum disperse heat quicker. Because they are thicker, new head studs .250" longer have to be installed along with the hardened flat washers to prevent the nuts from gouging into the head and to provide even torque. When using studs it is a good idea to coat them with "Neverseize" or "Coppercote" before installing the heads to prevent corrosion and make them easier to remove at a later date.

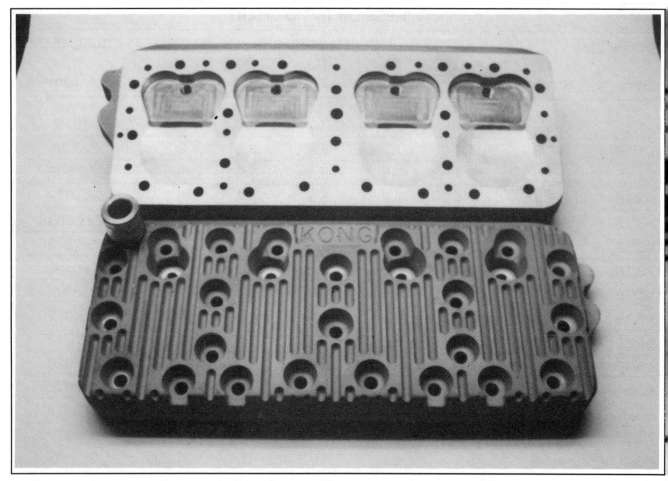

The Kong head with its much larger combustion chamber at .600" deep and measuring 76.2cc allows more flow around the valves especially at high RPM than its counterparts. While most cylinder heads have the spark plug located over the exhaust valve (the hottest part of the chamber) they are located in the center of the chamber in these heads. It probably would not make much difference to performance where the spark plug was located, but considering that these heads were designed for high performance, and in that application larger intake valves are usually fitted, they may have been better located closer to the exhaust valve allowing more clearance over the intake valve.

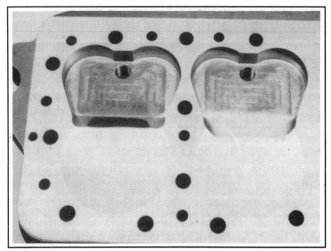

Here the modified combustion chamber can be seen which increased the volume to 78.6cc. The dome was then remachined to accept the Arias pistons increasing the volume to 89.2cc.

On the Race engine I am using Kong Heads which have a .600" valve clearance and differ from their counterparts in that the castings are 3/4" thick over the combustion chamber to allow for pop up pistons and high octane fuel. The combustion chamber is machined at 5° to match the inclination of the valves, and the spark plugs are located between the valves. With these heads I am using a .030" thick solid aluminum head gasket sprayed both sides with "Hylomar" to make them water tight as the engine will be fitted with a supercharger. The over the counter composition big bore head gaskets work fine in a naturally aspirated engine, but fail quickly under boost conditions. These heads were supplied with Allen head bolts which I prefer to use over studs as they will be removed on a regular basis for inspection.

The following tests were conducted on the same port as all previous tests using a Superflow

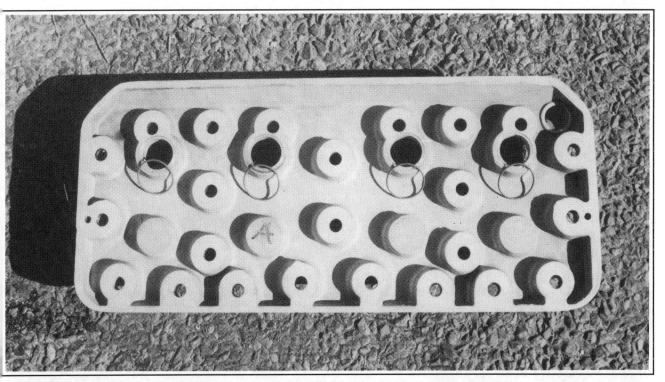

The Kong heads I am using are from the first batch of 15 sets that were sold in two piece configuration, necessitating another modification. The two halves were sealed with "Hylomar", but after several runs on the dyno they began to leak water around the spark plugs. The sealer broke down from combustion chamber heat requiring the top half of the heads to be machined to take .060" diameter Viton (high temperature) O rings.

110 flow bench I have recently installed in my shop. This makes for an interesting comparison between brands.

Offy .375 Head:

Lift:	.075	.150	.225	.300	.375	.450
CFM:	25.5	43.6	59.2	71.4	80.8	84

Offy .425 Head:

Lift:	.075	.150	.225	.300	.375	.450
CFM:	26.4	45.4	61.3	75.6	85	90.8

Navarro .450 Head:

Lift:	.075	.150	.225	.300	.375	.450
CFM:	26.8	46.6	63	77.7	87	93.8

Kong: .525 Head:

Lift:	.075	.150	.225	.300	.375	.450
CFM:	26.1	44.8	57.9	68	74.7	80.3

Kong .600 Head Modified:

Lift:	.075	.150	.225	.300	.375	.450
CFM:	28	48	63	76.1	85.5	91.3

Edelbrock .375 Head:

Lift:	.075	.150	.225	.300	.375	.450
CFM:	26.1	43.3	57.5	68.8	78.7	80.8

To best understand how the cylinder head works it must be divided into three sections. We already know that the more clearance there is around the valves in section A, the more flow will be obtained which can be seen in the comparison tests between the Offy heads. Even more important is section B where the flow is leaving the head and trying to get down the bore. Clear evidence of this can be seen in the comparison tests between the Kong heads. The contour of section C is directly related to the shape of the top of the piston.

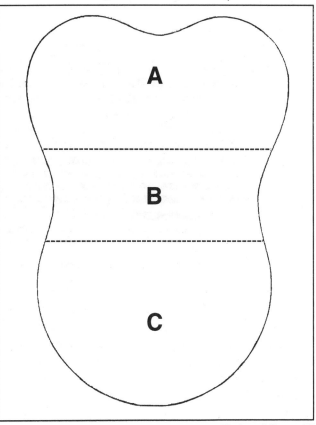

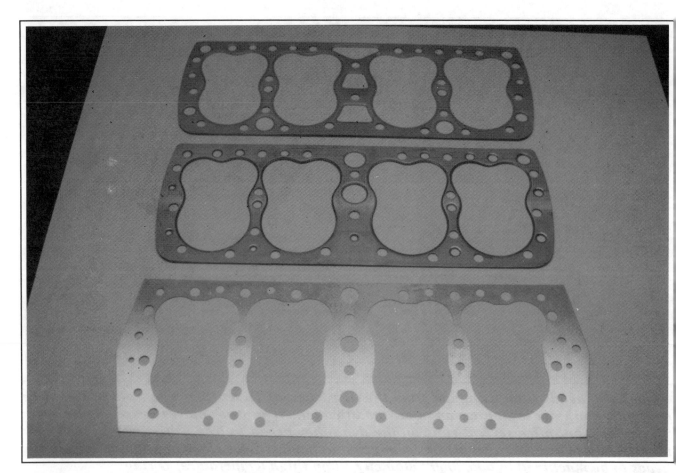

At the top is a McCord composition head gasket, very robust and a favourite of mine but unfortunately no longer available. In the center is a Victor Big Bore (up to 3-7/16" head gasket for an early engine. Felpro supply a similar gasket for late engines. At the bottom is a solid .030" thick aluminum gasket supplied by Kong Jackson and ideal for very high compression engines.

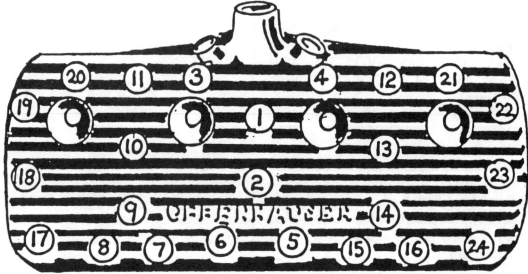

Whether using studs or bolts apply GM3835215 sealing compound to the threads as most of them go into the water jacket. A drop of oil should also be applied to either side of the flat washer, and if using studs, on the thread before installing the nut to provide even torque. When torquing down the cylinder heads this sequence should be followed and should be done in three stages alternating from side to side. After the engine has been initially run to bed in the cam and allowed to cool the heads should be re-torqued and again after 200-300 miles. Composition gaskets will compress quite a lot and I suggest torqueing to 55ft.lbs. while shim gaskets do not compress at all, and given the extra compression should be torqued to 65ft.lb.

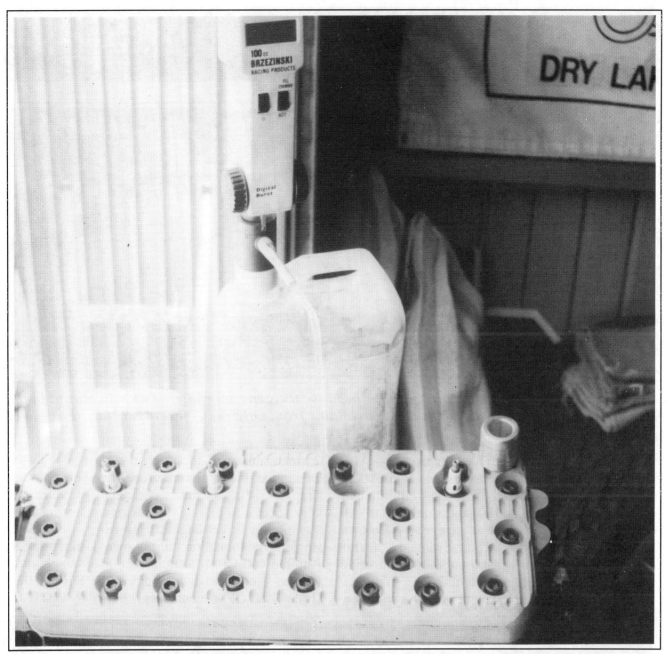

Accurately checking the compression ratio in a flathead engine can be difficult, but by using a Brzezinski digital Burette the task can be simplified. While the engine is still on the stand, tilt it until the bank of cylinders to be checked is level, and rotate the engine until the cylinder to be checked is at TDC. Smear a thin layer of petroleum jelly over everything including the deck/head surfaces. Install the gasket and cylinder head and fill with water from the burret to the bottom of the spark plug hole using the formula:-

$$\frac{22}{7} \times \frac{R}{1} \times \frac{R}{1} \times \frac{STROKE}{1}$$

= volume of 1 cylinder in cu. in.
x 16.3872
= cc's in 1 cylinder

$$\frac{swept\ volume + chamber\ volume}{chamber\ volume}$$
=compression ratio.

INTAKES

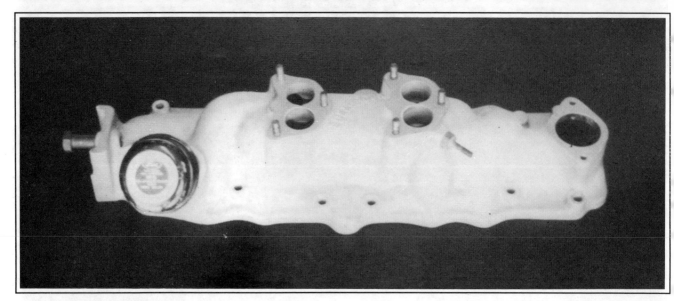

The regular dual intake is quite popular because the generator/alternator will mount in the stock location making it easy to fit and is available from Offenhauser and recently re-released by Sharp.

A book could be written on the many and varied intakes made for these engines, and at last count there were over 100. All these intakes fall into two categories, dual plane or 180° and single plane. All OEM intakes are dual plane as are most well known brands available today. The advantage of this design is the equal fuel distribution in conjunction with the firing order to each cylinder.

The single plane intake does not share the low down response of the dual plane, but does work well in the mid to high rev range and being a much simpler casting is much cheaper to produce and very popular in marine and racing applications.

On the street engine I am using a two piece single plane tunnel ram of my own design using an Autolite 600 CFM vacuum secondary single quad for the street, and by swapping the top use dual Holley 450 CFM mechanical secondary quads for

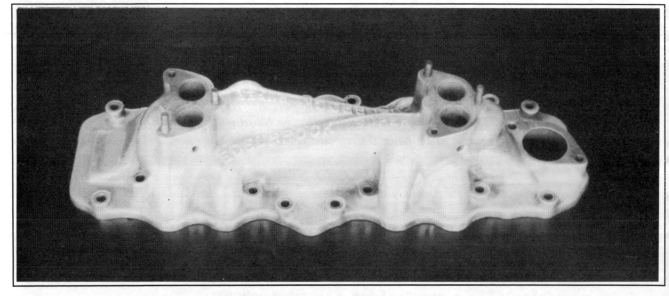

The super dual intake is more suited to a performance application with the carbs placed directly over the ports but necessitates the generator/alternator to be mounted above the cylinder head and is available from Offenhauser and recently re-released by Edelbrock and Sharp.

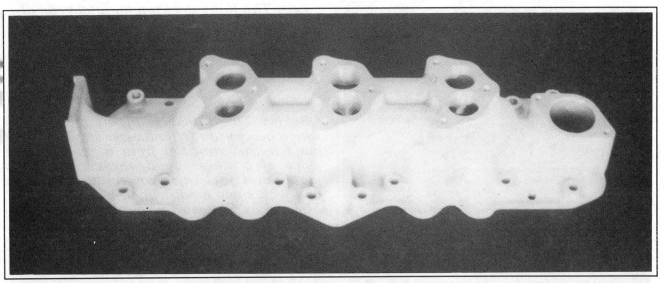

The triple intake was designed for performance in the larger capacity engines and is available from Offenhauser and Sharp. Linkage kits and offset generator brackets are available for all these multi carb configurations from Offenhauser.

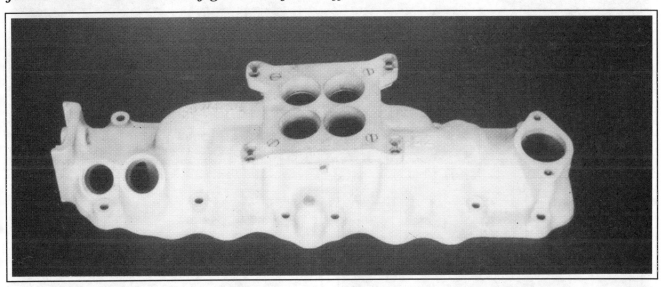

The single quad intake was released in the last production year of these engines as these newly designed carbs became available and with an adapter can be mated to more modern designed carbs. Although these intakes will fit all engines I would recommend only using them in late engines as the throttle interferes with the L/H water outlet hose on early cylinder heads. They are available from Offenhauser (who also supply the adapter) and Sharp.

the drags.

The race car will use a variety of intakes depending on the class:- Single 600 CFM mechanical secondary quad, dual 450 CFM mechanical secondary quads, B&M 162 cu. in. Supercharger overdriven 100% with a single 600 CFM mechanical secondary quad, and Air Sensors electronic fuel injection with and without the Supercharger. The supercharger is good for 9lb of boost.

Kong Jackson released this intake a few years ago which features a removable top allowing 2, 3 or 4 Stromberg carbs to be fitted.

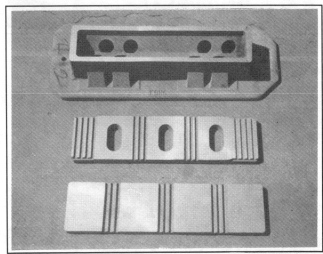

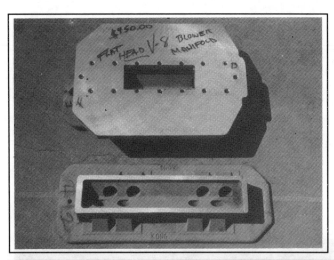

Left: The Kong Jackson manifold can also be supplied with an adaptor to suit a GM 4.71 or 6.71 supercharger.

Below: This intake is of my own design which accepts an Offenhauser single or dual quad tunnel ram top from a SB Chev. In place of a single quad, throttle body and multi-point fuel injection could be utilised and with some modification a supercharger. Motor City Flathead now offer a triple carb top for this manifold.

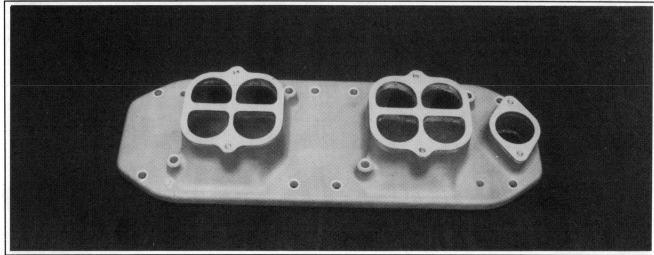

The same manifold with single quad top from a small block Chev manifold added.

The same manifold again but this time with dual quad top added.

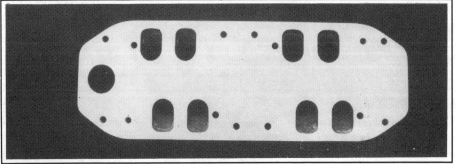

The underside shows the unique D ports, and they are available direct from myself or in the US from Motorcity Flathead.

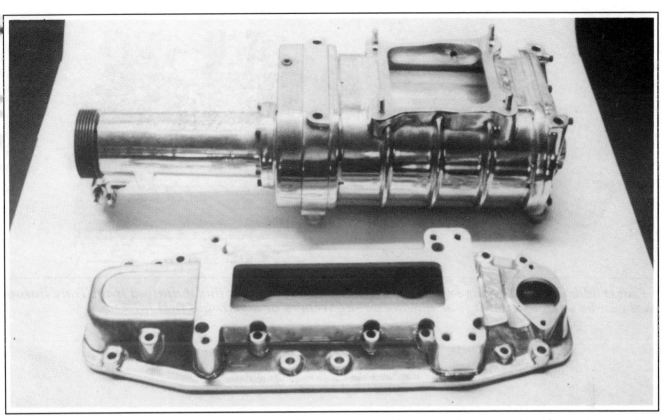

Several blower setups have been available for flatheads over the years but none as good as the B&M. Two sizes are available, 144 and 162 cu inch with a variety of pulley and belt combinations to meet all boost requirements and are available from Motorcity Flathead.

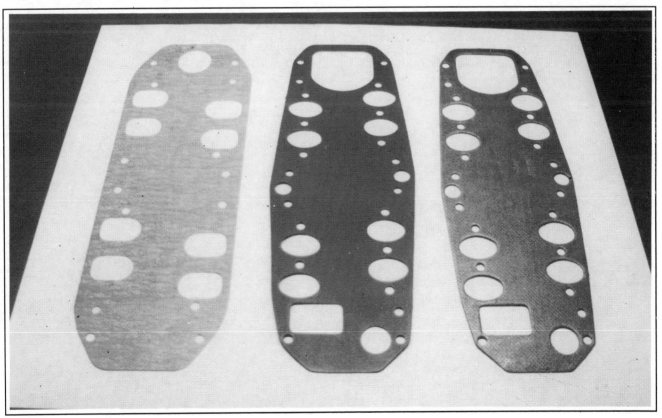

The gasket on the left is supplied with my own intake. Compare the size of the ports with the Offenhauser big port next to it and a Felpro replacement on the right. Also notice the lack of heat riser holes, as these should be blocked off with a piece of stainless steel shim or similar to prevent exhaust gas from heating the intake unless you live in a particularly cold climate.

Latest addition to the range of Flathead induction systems is this manifold from Tony Baron that can be used to mount four downdraught Webers or electronic fuel injection

IGNITIONS

It is no secret that Ford ignitions leave a lot to be desired. Over the years just about every combination imaginable has been tried, and whilst some are still available, advances in technology have resulted in much improved versions of old ignitions.

Mallory still make a mechanical advance dual point and more recently a Unilite distributor. MSD recently released a vacuum advanced magnetic pickup distributor while Vertex still make a magneto. All of these are suitable for 8BA's, while for the early engines Mallory has recently released a crab distributor in either dual point or Unilite with mechanical advance to fit two or three bolt timing covers, while a couple of sources supply Divers Helmet and Crab distributors modified with Allison Optical Trigger kits on a change over basis and the ever popular Harmon Collins magneto is being reproduced.

Some of these ignitions are quite expensive so for the budget minded there is an alternative. On 8BA engines the Chev V8 single point distributors work well requiring some machining on the housing and shaft and swapping drive gears. On the ear-

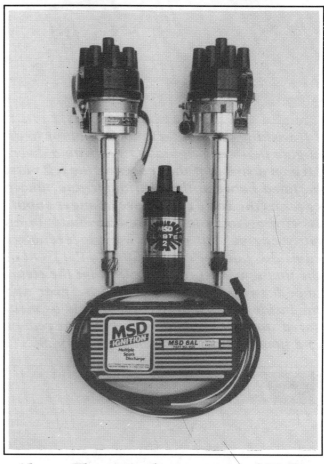

Above: These are the two types of Mallory distributors available. On the left is the Unilite which should be used in conjunction with a resistor reducing distributor voltage from 12 to 9 eliminating the possibility of damaging the triggering source.

Below: This is a crab distributor I have modified using Echlin LS777A points and FA77 condensor. I also remove the vacuum brake because it is not necessary with today's higher octane fuels, and if the engine is being used in a performance application remove the counterweights as well, giving full advance off idle.

If wishing to install a crab distributor to an engine that was originally fitted with a divers Helmet distributor the spacer on the left must be fitted between the distributor and timing cover as the early cams have a longer snout. If wishing to install a late distributor to an early engine, but do not want to exchange cams this adapter can be fitted to the front of the timing gear. In this application the clearance between the distributor drive gear and the inside of the timing cover should be measured and a cam button installed to reduce end float of the cam to not more than .005".

lier engines I have had success with modifying Crab distributors using a modern condensor and single points.

Regardless of the type of ignition used, I would recommend fabricating a timing pointer and attaching it to the timing cover (8BA engines have these standard) and using a file make notches on the front pulley so that the timing can be set with a timing light.

For the street engine I am using Mallory twin point with an MSD 6A, MSD Blaster coil, Taylor 8mm high tension leads with NGK B6HS spark plugs set at .032. These distributors are factory pre-set at 24° total advance which is perfect for this application but can be adjusted and a special tool is included for this purpose.

For the race car I am using a Mallory Unilite with MSD 6AL (rev control), MSD Blaster coil, Taylor 8mm high tension leads with NGK B9ES spark plugs set at .032". This distributor is also a mechanical advance but because the car is used in four classes using different induction setups and fuels an MSD adjustable timer control is fitted.

The timing gear on the left is from an early engine where the thrust is directed towards the block. If wishing to fit a late distributor to an early engine the late crank and timing gear must also be fitted directing the thrust towards the timing cover.

EXHAUST

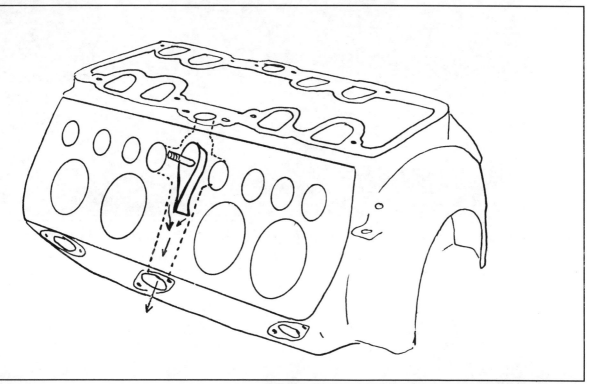

The exhaust is probably the worst design feature of these engines being inefficient and the reason they run so hot.

Cadillac had the right idea by running the exhaust out the top of the block between the intake ports and this idea has been copied by a few racers over the years with success, but is a lot of work not to mention the expense.

Ford realised the problem of two cylinders using the same port and on the Lincoln cast in a divider, but not so on these engines. Bolt in port dividers are available over the counter, or they can be fabricated from 1/8" plate and arc welded in via the heat riser hole. The reason they are so important is because the firing order between the centre cylinders is 180° apart so while the exhaust valve is closing the intake valve next to it is opening drawing the spent gas back into the cylinder diluting the mixture.

Both engines are fitted with reproduction Belond headers which compliment the shape of the exhaust ports having 1-3/4" primary pipes going into a 2-1/2" collector. On the race car engine they have been HPC coated inside and out, which not only stops them corroding, but directs the heat down the pipe rather than through it to make them scavenge more efficiently and make horsepower.

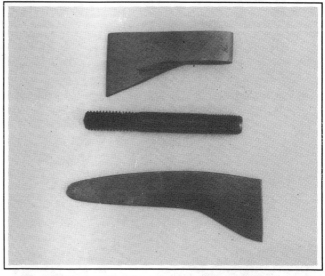

The bolt in divider (above) is held in position with long nose pliers while the countersunk hole in the top is lined up with the stud hole in the block. The stud is then fitted clamping the divider in place. Simple, but effective. The weld in divider must be individually fitted to each side of the block (as castings do vary) and welded through the heat riser hole and on either side to the floor of the port with a stainless steel rod. A time consuming job that can only be done with the valves removed.

The centre exhaust ports have been enlarged to 1-9/16" and the end ports have been elongated as much as it practical. Some racers go to a lot of work to straighten the end ports, but in most instances the added gains are not worth the effort, requiring custom made headers.

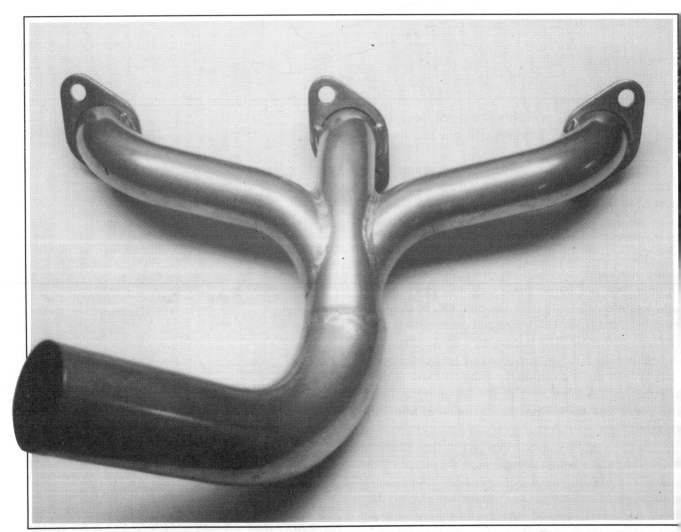

This is a reproduction of the popular Belond header of the fifties, which is basically a fabricated copy of the cast Miller Ford header of the thirties. They are well made but require some cleaning up on the inside and will fit most applications.

COOLING

Knowing what water pump fitted which engine can make identifying an engine easier. Top left – single pulley passenger car pump used between 1937-48, lubricated directly from the engine's oiling system. Top right – double pulley truck pump used between 1937-48, has a double row sealed bearing, but shares the same seal as the passenger car pump. Bottom left – 1949 passenger car and 1949-54 pickup shared this pump having an externally lubricated bush and single row bearing with modern neoprene seal, but no provision for mounting. Bottom centre – 1950-54 passenger car pump is identical to the previous pump with the inclusion of a mounting pad. Bottom right – 1949-54 truck pump has a double row sealed bearing with a mounting pad identical to the 1937-48 pumps.

Keeping a Flathead cool is a tough job!

By overboring and raising the compression the problem only gets worse. There is some degree of tradeoff by fitting aluminium heads and dual exhaust, but gains can be made by fitting the largest possible radiator as this is one area that has improved over the years with much more efficient core design.

It is essential that two thermostats are fitted rather than two washers with small holes in them or

Conversion kit as marketed by the author has a modified impellor and modern seal as shown at left in the photo. On the right is the OEM replacement kit.

On 8BA engines the 7/16" hole above the impellor should be blocked in either the block or the pump to prevent heated water from the cylinder head mixing with cooled water being pumped from the radiator.

The 348/409 Chev water pump and saddle. This saddle has had the mounts removed and replaced with fabricated ones that are mounted lower to give a cleaner appearance on the street engine.

nothing at all. The thermostats will allow the engine to warm up quickly by remaining closed and when warm will open enough to keep the temperature constant by acting as a restrictor to slow the flow of water down so it spends enought time in the radiator to cool.

On 8BA engines the water pumps use a mod-

ern seal and work reasonably well, whereas with the early water pumps the seal is of an antiquated design that did not work particularly well in years gone by, and no better now. To improve on this I have designed a conversion kit with a modified impellor and modern seal which overcomes the problem of premature leaking while the shaft is

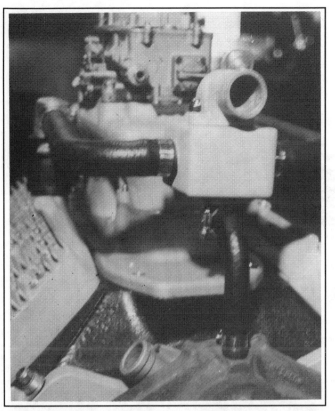

Left & Below: On the street engine the pump is driven in the conventional way with the water hoses coming from the cylinder heads meeting in a junction box above the pump which is connected via a short piece of heater hose and houses a bypass thermostat. These differ from the conventional thermostats in that water circulates through the engine constantly until normal operating temperature is reached when the thermostat opens, closing off the bypass and normal circulation takes over. The advantages of this concept is to keep the temperature more constant throughout the engine eliminating hot spots. A coolant-recovery system will also be incorporated with this.

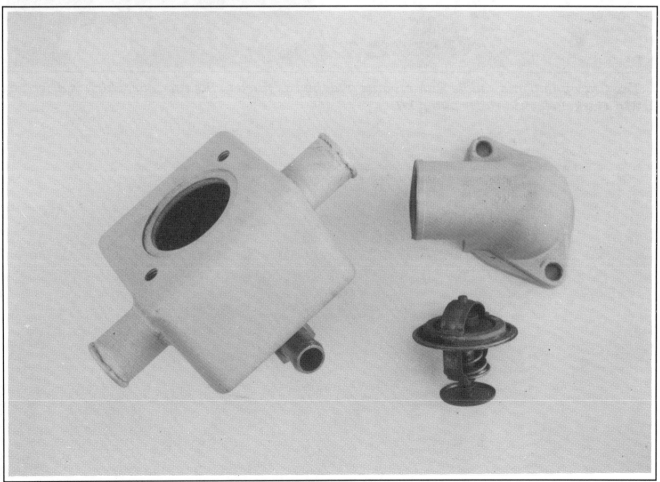

drilled and fitted with a grease nipple to provide additional lubrication. The truck version of this pump has a double row bearing and does not suffer from lack of lubrication.

See attached photo.

On both engines I have taken this a step further by casting saddle mounts to which I have attached a 348/409 Chev water pump.

The Chev pump and saddle with mounts attached as fitted to the race car which is driven by a Mr. Gasket electric water pump kit.

TRANSMISSIONS

I doubt whether anyone who has driven an early Ford for any length of time would compliment the transmission. Basically they are not very strong and any attempt to change gears in a hurry results in continued grating. Fortunately, there are several adapters available to make fitting modern transmissions easy.

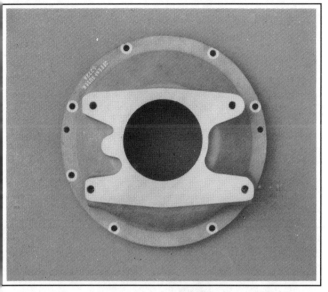

On early engines the Offenhauser 5272 adapter enables the Saginaw 3 and 4 speed and Muncie 4 speed transmissions to be fitted and by using a 5272A in conjunction with a 5204 a Toploader 3 or 4 speed can be fitted.

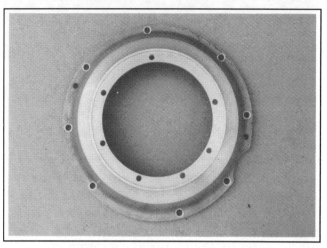

Another of my adaptors mates a powerglide auto to an early engine. Powerglides were sold in Australia behind Chev V8's in full size passenger cars, but in 1965 GM supplied them in the medium sized six cylinder powered passenger cars by chopping off the front of the bellhousing and making one of their own. By 1967 a new case had been produced to match the existing bellhousing which this adaptor fits. The advantage of using the 6 cylinder internals is the better 1st gear ratio of 1.82 as compared to the V8 1.76 and by using the V8 4 clutch pack instead of the 6 cylinder 3 clutch pack an unbreakable combination is achieved which is especially suited to light weight and competition vehicles.

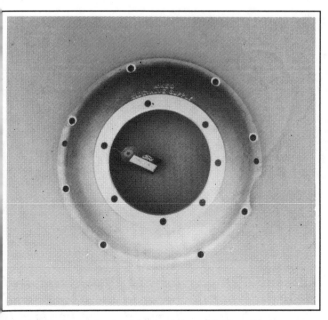

This adapter produced by the author mates the popular C4 auto to early engines.

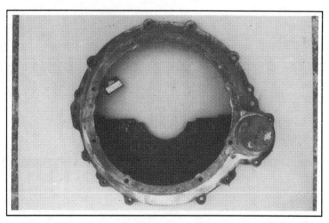

The 8BA truck adapter is a sought after item allowing adapters designed for early engines to be fitted to later ones. This bellhousing was made of cast iron and is able to accept an 11" clutch. The same bellhousing was available in pressed steel in the Mercury but it would only accept a 10" clutch.

Above: 8BA passenger car bellhousings can be modified to accept a toploader 3 and 4 speed by enlarging the bearing retainer hole. Pictured is a 1949 pressed steel unit which surely must be the original scattershield.

Right: The powerglide and adapter is dummied up behind the street engine during initial assembly. With this setup the original 6 cylinder torque converter is also retained.

The Saginaw 4 speed with Hurst shifter, Offenhauser 5272A adaptor and safety shield used in the race car. The safety shield is 5/8" thick mild steel that fits between the adaptor and engine block with a 1/4" thick shroud to contain the clutch should it explode. The flywheel is made from 1" thick billet aluminum with a steel insert weighing 15lbs while the pressure plate is an 11" truck unit and an 11" Chev clutch plate.

While not really related to transmissions the starter motors shown are compatible with the respective engines and adaptors previously listed.

Top – This starter is made by Lucas and was supplied on all Pilot passenger cars and Thames trucks imported from England to Australia between 1946-50. The body is 1" shorter and the shaft 1" longer than the American equivalent with a 144 tooth ring gear. I am using these starters on both my cars as they allow more clearance around the headers and for this reason are easier to remove and install.

Centre – early starter, 112 tooth ring gear.

Bottom – 8BA starter, 112 tooth ring gear.

Almost all flatheads were equipped with 6 volt ignitions and if the starter is in good condition will give years of trouble-free service on 12 volts without any modification. I haven't checked either of the American starters, but the Lucas will spin the engine at 230 rpm.

The street engine is shown here in the dyno room ready to be fired up for testing.

any longer), and then drained and refilled with Penrite turbo oil (25-70). Premium unleaded fuel with an octane rating of 96 delivered at 7 PSI was used in all naturally aspirated tests. Unleaded fuel is preferred because the oxygen sensor connected to the exhaust is susceptible to premature failure when used with leaded fuel.

After the initial run-in period the engine was allowed to cool and the heads retorqued. From the first run it was obvious there was a fuel distribution problem. To overcome this the power valve was removed and the carb square jetted. A slight improvement was noticed but after several jet changes we were not making any headway, the oxygen sensor saying one thing and the plugs saying the opposite with poor horsepower figures. (SEE TEST NO. 23).

At this time it seemed appropriate to thumb through the book Super Tuning and Modifying Holley Carburetors by Dave Emanuel in which he states "ram manifolds with a single carb may look

---

Test No. 23

Test 500 rpm Step Test	Fuel Spec. Grav.:	.768	Air Sensor:	6.5
Vapor Pressure: .46	Barometric Pressure.:	29.94	Ratio:	1.00 TO 1
Engine Type: 4 Cycle Spark	Engine Displacement:	284.0	Stroke:	4.125

Speed RPM	C.P. Trq. lb-ft	C.P. Pwr. Hp	FHp Hp	VE%	ME%	FA lb/hr	A1 scfm	A/F	BSFC lb/Hphr	CAT	Oil	Wat.	BSAC lb/Hphr
3000	185.3	105.8	28.2	.0	78.2	67.2	.0	.0	.66	81	0	173	.00
3500	207.1	138.0	37.2	.0	78.0	87.7	.0	.0	.67	84	0	170	.00
4000	209.7	159.7	47.1	.0	76.5	95.9	.0	.0	.63	79	0	170	.00
4500	214.2	183.5	57.9	.0	75.1	137.3	.0	.0	.78	82	0	176	.00
5000	185.9	177.0	70.0	.0	70.7	83.4	.0	.0	.49	80	0	176	.00

25° Advance   66 Jets   Holley 600 Double Pumper

Throughout this book I have described what modifications have been made to the street engine, followed by the race engine. In fact the race engine was completed and tested first. The engine, fitted with the single quad high rise and Holley 600 double pumper carb was installed on a Superflow 901 Dyno.

At this time I should mention several points – The engine was filled with Penrite running in oil for the initial run-in period of 30 minutes (an engine with large clearance such as this does not require

impressive, but fuel distribution problems plague such installations." More on this problem later.

The dual quads were then installed and instantly the fuel distribution problems were solved. After a couple of jet changes the best run was recorded on TEST NO. 36. Up to this time several changes in ignition timing had been tried with 25° total advance at 3,000 RPM producing the most horsepower.

The supercharger was then fitted and I should mention that this engine was primarily designed for

Test No. 36

Test 500 rpm Step Test	Fuel Spec. Grav.:	.768	Air Sensor:	6.5
Vapor Pressure: .46	Barometric Pressure.:	29.93	Ratio:	1.00 TO 1
Engine Type: 4 Cycle Spark	Engine Displacement:	284.0	Stroke:	4.125

Speed RPM	C.P. Trq. lb-ft	C.P. Pwr. Hp	FHp Hp	VE%	ME%	FA lb/hr	A1 scfm	A/F	BSFC lb/Hphr	CAT	Oil	Wat.	BSAC lb/Hphr
3000	217.0	124.0	28.2	.0	80.9	63.3	.0	.0	.53	77	0	199	.00
3500	225.1	150.0	37.2	.0	79.5	79.4	.0	.0	.55	76	0	201	.00
4000	233.7	178.0	47.1	.0	78.4	90.6	.0	.0	.53	77	0	201	.00
4500	231.9	198.7	57.9	.0	76.7	102.0	.0	.0	.54	78	0	202	.00
5000	219.6	209.1	70.0	.0	74.1	111.2	.0	.0	.56	78	0	203	.00

25° Advance   55 Secondary Jets, 57 Primary Jets   Dual Quad Economasters

Test No. 56

Test 500 rpm Step Test	Fuel Spec. Grav.:	.768	Air Sensor:	6.5
Vapor Pressure: .46	Barometric Pressure.:	29.75	Ratio:	1.00 TO 1
Engine Type: 4 Cycle Spark	Engine Displacement:	284.0	Stroke:	4.125

Speed RPM	C.P. Trq. lb-ft	C.P. Pwr. Hp	FHp Hp	VE%	ME%	FA lb/hr	A1 scfm	A/F	BSFC lb/Hphr	CAT	Oil	Wat.	BSAC lb/Hphr
3500	330.3	220.1	37.2	.0	85.0	131.2	.0	.0	.62	76	0	160	.00
4000	336.4	256.2	47.1	.0	83.9	151.1	.0	.0	.61	74	0	163	.00
4500	331.8	284.3	57.9	.0	82.5	175.8	.0	.0	.65	75	0	168	.00
5000	315.0	299.9	70.0	.0	80.4	200.1	.0	.0	.70	75	0	169	.00
5500	290.8	304.5	95.6	.0	77.3	199.7	.0	.0	.69	74	0	182	.00

10° Advance   76 Front Jets, 75 Rear Jets   600 Double Pumper

this application and has a compression ratio of 8.15:1, hence the relatively low horsepower figures achieved up to this time. The Holley 600 double pumper was reinstalled and after several jet changes the best run was recorded on TEST NO. 56. As the effective compression ratio under boost is close to 13:1 the timing was retarded continually until we settled on 10° total advance at 3,000 RPM. During these runs we had been checking plugs regularly for signs of detonation which shows up in the form of pin prick size black spots on the porcelain and although we had initially seen them, were now confident we were safe.

With the tests now complete, a leakdown check was performed on all cylinders to gauge how good the rings sealed and they were all within three pounds except one. After removing the cylinder head it was obvious the detonation previously experienced was worse than first thought as the gasket was eaten away on the lower half of each piston, leaving a jagged saw tooth effect with a piece miss-

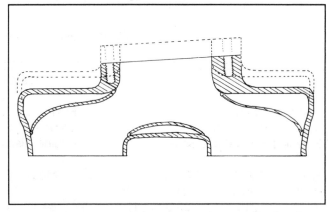

This diagram shows how the single high rise manifold was modified internally to improve the fuel distribution and to speed up the airflow.

ing completely in one cylinder.

The street engine fitted with the single quad high rise (modified) and Autolite 600 vacuum secondary carb was installed on the dyno. This engine was also filled with Penrite running-in oil for the initial run-in period of one hour and then drained and refilled with Penrite HPR30 oil (25-60).

This engine has a compression ratio of 9:1 and is also using Premium unleaded fuel delivered at 5 PSI.

After the initial run-in period the engine was allowed to cool and the heads re-torqued. The best run was recorded on TEST NO. 15 with the timing set at 25° total advance at 3,000 RPM which was found to be the most suitable on all runs.

The dual quads were then installed with the best run recorded on TEST NO. 12. As both torque and horsepower were down it is obvious that the carbs are too big for this engine. In the past I have used this set up on two engines, one at 281 cubic inches and the other at 284 cubic inches and they worked very well so I would suggest that this is the cut off point. An interesting comparison would be to try dual Holley 350 two barrels or dual Holley 390 four barrel vacuum secondary carbs.

The Holley 600 double pumper was then installed as I wanted a back to back comparison with the modified and unmodified single quad top. TEST NO. 7 is with the modified top and TEST NO. 8 is with the unmodified top. In deciding how to go about modifying the top I had two options, to design a new top or modify the existing one. It was much cheaper to modify the original so I cut it in half, removed the divider that ran its full length and added the curved plates to better direct the mixture and reduce the overall internal area to speed up the airflow. See attached diagram. Another jet change was made and the best run was recorded in TEST NO. 28.

TEST NO. 23 – 66 jets all round.
TEST NO. 36 – 57 primary, 55 secondary jets.
TEST NO. 56 – 76 primary, 75 secondary jets.
Note the exhaust temperature which is 1230°F.

Optimum temperature for an engine is between 1250°-1350°F and although you cannot tune an engine by exhaust temperature alone it is a

---

Test No. 15

Test 500 rpm Step Test	Fuel Spec. Grav.:	.768	Air Sensor:	6.5
Vapor Pressure: .45	Barometric Pressure.:	30.21	Ratio:	1.00 TO 1
Engine Type: 4 Cycle Spark	Engine Displacement:	276.0	Stroke:	4.000

Speed RPM	C.P. Trq. lb-ft	C.P. Pwr. Hp	FHp Hp	VE%	ME%	FA lb/hr	A1 scfm	A/F	BSFC lb/Hphr	CAT	Oil	Wat.	BSAC lb/Hphr
2250	198.2	84.9	17.1	.0	82.9	56.9	.0	.0	.68	72	0	193	.00
2750	222.9	116.7	23.4	.0	83.0	60.7	.0	.0	.53	72	0	193	.00
3250	224.0	138.6	30.9	.0	81.5	76.4	.0	.0	.56	73	0	193	.00
3750	232.6	166.1	39.9	.0	80.3	84.9	.0	.0	.52	74	0	194	.00
4250	221.9	179.6	49.7	.0	77.9	93.0	.0	.0	.53	75	0	196	.00
4750	207.2	187.4	60.5	.0	75.1	101.4	.0	.0	.56	75	0	198	.00
5250	186.3	186.2	72.4	.0	71.5	108.4	.0	.0	.60	73	0	200	.00

25° Advance   55 Front Jets, 70 Rear Jets.   Autolite 600 Vac. Sec.

Test No. 12

Test 500 rpm Step Test	Fuel Spec. Grav.:	.768	Air Sensor:	6.5
Vapor Pressure: .45	Barometric Pressure.:	30.24	Ratio:	1.00 TO 1
Engine Type: 4 Cycle Spark	Engine Displacement:	276.0	Stroke:	4.000

Speed RPM	C.P. Trq. lb-ft	C.P. Pwr. Hp	FHp Hp	VE%	ME%	FA lb/hr	A1 scfm	A/F	BSFC lb/Hphr	CAT	Oil	Wat.	BSAC lb/Hphr
2250	215.5	92.3	17.1	.0	84.1	54.4	.0	.0	.60	70	0	197	.00
2750	221.6	116.0	23.4	.0	83.1	64.5	.0	.0	.56	65	0	198	.00
3250	223.4	138.2	30.9	.0	81.5	75.9	.0	.0	.56	70	0	199	.00
3750	222.9	159.2	39.9	.0	79.7	87.2	.0	.0	.56	68	0	198	.00
4250	212.3	171.8	49.7	.0	77.3	97.8	.0	.0	.58	70	0	198	.00
4750	201.7	182.4	60.5	.0	74.7	107.5	.0	.0	.60	71	0	199	.00
5250	182.4	182.3	72.4	.0	71.2	115.4	.0	.0	.65	71	0	199	.00

25° Advance   57 Front Jets, 61 Rear Jets.   Dual Quad Economasters

Test No. 7

Test 500 rpm Step Test   Fuel Spec. Grav.:   .768   Air Sensor: 6.5
Vapor Pressure: .45   Barometric Pressure.:   30.25   Ratio: 1.00 TO 1
Engine Type: 4 Cycle Spark   Engine Displacement: 276.0   Stroke: 4.000

Speed RPM	C.P. Trq. lb-ft	C.P. Pwr. Hp	FHp Hp	VE%	ME%	FA lb/hr	A1 scfm	A/F	BSFC lb/Hphr	CAT	Oil	Wat.	BSAC lb/Hphr
2000	186.2	70.9	14.4	.0	82.9	51.5	.0	.0	.74	70	0	187	.00
2500	219.9	104.7	20.1	.0	83.7	68.8	.0	.0	.67	70	0	191	.00
3000	226.5	129.4	26.8	.0	82.6	76.5	.0	.0	.60	71	0	192	.00
3500	233.0	155.3	35.3	.0	81.3	86.6	.0	.0	.57	69	0	192	.00
4000	227.6	173.3	44.7	.0	79.3	95.9	.0	.0	.56	67	0	193	.00
4500	211.8	181.5	55.0	.0	76.6	106.5	.0	.0	.59	64	0	194	.00
5000	196.5	187.1	66.4	.0	73.4	117.7	.0	.0	.64	70	0	197	.00

25° Advance   72 Front Jets, 72 Rear Jets.   600 Double Pumper

Test No. 8

Test 500 rpm Step Test   Fuel Spec. Grav.:   .768   Air Sensor: 6.5
Vapor Pressure: .45   Barometric Pressure.:   30.25   Ratio: 1.00 TO 1
Engine Type: 4 Cycle Spark   Engine Displacement: 276.0   Stroke: 4.000

Speed RPM	C.P. Trq. lb-ft	C.P. Pwr. Hp	FHp Hp	VE%	ME%	FA lb/hr	A1 scfm	A/F	BSFC lb/Hphr	CAT	Oil	Wat.	BSAC lb/Hphr
2000	154.6	58.9	14.4	.0	80.1	56.9	.0	.0	.99	74	0	194	.00
2500	169.0	80.4	20.1	.0	79.6	63.3	.0	.0	.80	74	0	195	.00
3000	195.8	111.8	26.8	.0	80.4	75.2	.0	.0	.68	72	0	191	.00
3500	201.4	134.2	35.3	.0	78.8	87.9	.0	.0	.67	75	0	193	.00
4000	209.4	159.5	44.7	.0	77.7	98.7	.0	.0	.63	75	0	195	.00
4500	196.1	168.0	55.0	.0	74.9	107.6	.0	.0	.65	73	0	193	.00
5000	174.3	165.9	66.4	.0	70.9	114.5	.0	.0	.71	74	0	200	.00

25° Advance   72 Front Jets, 72 Rear Jets.   600 Double Pumper

Test No. 28

Test 500 rpm Step Test   Fuel Spec. Grav.:   .768   Air Sensor: 6.5
Vapor Pressure: .45   Barometric Pressure.:   30.19   Ratio: 1.00 TO 1
Engine Type: 4 Cycle Spark   Engine Displacement: 276.0   Stroke: 4.000

Speed RPM	C.P. Trq. lb-ft	C.P. Pwr. Hp	FHp Hp	VE%	ME%	FA lb/hr	A1 scfm	A/F	BSFC lb/Hphr	CAT	Oil	Wat.	BSAC lb/Hphr
2250	193.1	92.7	17.1	.0	82.6	53.7	.0	.0	.66	68	0	195	.00
2750	236.5	123.8	23.4	.0	83.9	69.1	.0	.0	.57	69	0	196	.00
3250	241.3	149.3	30.9	.0	82.6	78.6	.0	.0	.53	67	0	196	.00
3750	240.6	171.8	39.9	.0	80.9	87.7	.0	.0	.52	67	0	193	.00
4250	228.5	184.9	49.7	.0	78.6	98.9	.0	.0	.54	67	0	197	.00
4750	216.0	195.4	60.5	.0	76.1	110.9	.0	.0	.58	67	0	198	.00
5250	194.7	194.6	72.4	.0	72.5	122.4	.0	.0	.64	68	0	200	.00

25° Advance   70 Front Jets, 72 Rear Jets.   600 Double Pumper

Test No. 57

Test: 200 r.p.m./sec. acceleration				Fuel Spec. Grav.:		.768			Air Sensor:				6.5
Vapor Pressure: .46				Barometric Pressure.:		29.75			Ratio:				1.00 TO 1
Engine Type: 4 Cycle Spark				Engine Displacement:		284.0			Stroke:				4.125

Speed RPM	C.P. Trq. lb-ft	C.P. Pwr. Hp	FHp Hp	VE%	ME%	FA lb/hr	A1 scfm	A/F	BSFC lb/Hphr	CAT	Oil	Wat.	BSAC lb/Hphr
2500	281.1	133.8	21.1	.0	85.9	99.8	.0	.0	.78	75	0	169	.00
2750	288.7	151.2	24.5	.0	85.6	108.2	.0	.0	.78	75	0	168	.00
3000	305.9	174.7	28.2	.0	85.6	133.5	.0	.0	.80	75	0	172	.00
3250	313.2	193.8	32.5	.0	85.1	125.6	.0	.0	.68	75	0	171	.00
3500	322.2	214.7	37.2	.0	84.7	124.9	.0	.0	.61	75	0	171	.00
3750	324.8	231.9	42.0	.0	84.1	159.7	.0	.0	.72	74	0	172	.00
4000	327.5	249.4	47.1	.0	83.6	145.5	.0	.0	.61	74	0	173	.00
4250	328.0	265.4	52.4	.0	82.9	164.0	.0	.0	.64	74	0	175	.00
4500	325.8	279.2	57.9	.0	82.2	177.3	.0	.0	.66	76	0	176	.00
4750	319.3	288.8	63.9	.0	81.2	189.7	.0	.0	.69	76	0	179	.00
5000	311.0	296.1	70.0	.0	80.2	199.9	.0	.0	.71	76	0	179	.00
5250	299.8	299.7	77.3	.0	78.8	231.8	.0	.0	.81	74	0	182	.00
5500	283.7	297.1	85.6	.0	76.8	261.6	.0	.0	.92	75	0	185	.00

10° Advance   76 Front Jets, 75 Rear Jets.   600 Double Pumper

good indicator that it is making horsepower.

TEST NO. 57 – This is an acceleration run, where previously the engine accelerates and is held at the given RPM for five seconds and recorded, while with this test it revs freely. You will note that the figures are slightly lower as it uses horsepower to accelerate.

TEST NO. 15 – 55 primary, 70 secondary jets.
TEST NO. 12 – 57 primary, 61 secondary jets.
TEST NO. 7 – 72 primary, 72 secondary jets.
TEST NO. 8 – 72 primary, 72 secondary jets.
TEST NO. 28 – 70 primary, 72 secondary jets.

Note the difference in mixture (BSFC) between TEST 7 and 8. Optimum should be between 55-60. Also note the water temperature on TEST NO. 28. Optimum horsepower is reached at approximately 205°F. You will notice in TEST NO. 56 the water temperature was quite cool as the hotter it becomes the more likely detonation is to occur.

Preliminary testing was carried out in the race car, reaching a top speed of 145 m.p.h. before mechanical problems surfaced. The engine was later disassembled whereupon I decided to alter the shape of the valve relief (see attached photo), machining to a depth of 0.120" and modifying the cylinder heads to suit (see cylinder head comparison chart). The intake valve seats were recut using a Mira 110B form cutter and the intake valves faced.

The engine was reassembled and reinstalled on the dyno with results as shown in Test No. 17.

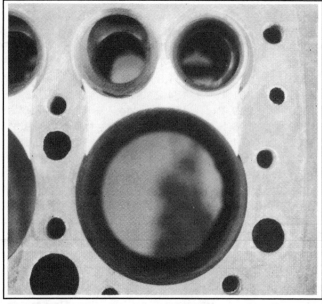

After testing in race conditions the engine was disassembled and the valve relief machined to a depth of 0.120".

For these tests the engine was fitted with a knock sensor as detonation was a major problem previously and I wanted to keep a close watch on what was happening. The knock sensor is a very sensitive instrument and will pick up any vibration and although I cannot be sure I believe it also picked up the vibration of the supercharger which would mask the symptons.

As the engine reached 4,500 r.p.m. the gauge moved from green to yellow, at 5,000 r.p.m. it was in the red and by 5,500 r.p.m. it was well into the

Test No. 17

Test: Data recorded manually					Fuel Spec. Grav.:			.731			Air Sensor:		6.5
Vapor Pressure: .46					Barometric Pressure.:			30.09			Ratio:		1.00 TO 1
Engine Type: 4 Cycle Spark					Engine Displacement:			284.0			Stroke:		4.125

Speed RPM	C.P. Trq. lb-ft	C.P. Pwr. Hp	FHp Hp	VE%	ME%	FA lb/hr	A1 scfm	A/F	BSFC lb/Hphr	CAT	Oil	Wat.	BSAC lb/Hphr
2500	293.6	139.9	21.1	.0	86.4	88.6	.0	.0	.66	88	0	176	.00
3000	313.3	179.0	28.2	.0	85.9	107.5	.0	.0	.63	88	0	178	.00
3500	325.7	217.1	37.2	.0	84.9	127.1	.0	.0	.61	87	0	180	.00
4000	330.6	251.8	47.1	.0	83.7	153.2	.0	.0	.63	86	0	183	.00
4500	324.5	278.0	57.9	.0	82.2	173.5	.0	.0	.65	86	0	186	.00
5000	311.1	296.2	70.0	.0	80.2	192.4	.0	.0	.68	87	0	190	.00
5500	293.2	307.0	85.6	.0	77.4	207.8	.0	.0	.71	88	0	199	.00

15° Advance   77 Front Jets, 77 Rear Jets.   600 Double Pumper

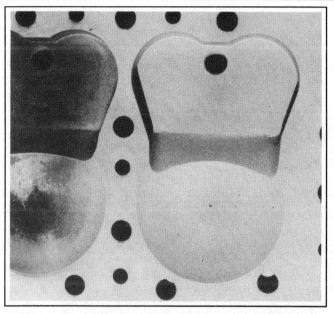

The cylinder heads were also modified for increased flow as shown here. The engine was then reassembled and dyno tested to reveal the results shown above.

red. A look at the spark plugs confirmed all was well.

To give a margin of safety the carburettor was jetted 77 square which was as rich as I could go without hurting performance.

For these tests I used Unical 76 Nascar fuel with an octane rating of 112. This allowed me to advance the timing to 15° total at 3,000 r.p.m. while exhaust temperature was a cool 1070°F.

The results in TEST NO.17 are not any better than previous tests but a larger degree of safety has been achieved.

SUMMARY

I have deliberately used components in the street engine that have been available for more than forty years, other than the induction and ignition, to show the potential of the engine in a format that the average hot rodder can appreciate and afford.

The race car engine is a different story. The lessons learnt on the previous engine have been incorporated along with the best components available for the engine to not only make a lot of horsepower, but stay together. At four times the price of the street engine it has ceased to be an alternative to all but the serious flathead racer.

Further testing was carried out at the D.L.R.A. speed trials on Lake Gairdner in March 1995 with a top speed of 162 m.p.h. Future improvements include a long overdue belly pan and to substitute Air Sensors electronic fuel injection for the Holley carb., plus the addition of nitrous oxide injection. The supercharger, currently overdriven 200% will be stepped up to 220% to try for 180 m.p.h.

At this point the car will be rebodied with a chopped and stretched Fiat Topolino body and it is hoped in this format I can reach my goal of 200 m.p.h.

CONCLUSION

As this book is in its second print I thought it would provide an opportunity to reflect on how the two engines have performed.

The hot rod is now registered and providing a lot of fun. I have fitted the Autolite carby for more economy on the street and after my initial test drive I found it necessary to fit a choke. The engine and in particular the plenum, requires a few minutes warm up from a cold start and upon reaching operating temperature idles quite smoothly at 850 RPM and 750 RPM in gear. On hard acceleration I have no trouble in lighting up the tyres and again when shifting into high gear. In fact the engine has so much torque it will pull away from a standstill at full throttle in high gear with hesitation.

As a requirement for registration in South Australia I had to submit the hot rod for a lane change test as the front track is more than two inches narrower than the rear. The test is set up to comply with International Standards where you must drive through three sets of cones maintaining 80 kph (50 mph), but in this state we are required to go 110 kph (68mph). The test was conducted at the local raceway with two engineers to observe, with a device fitted to the windshield to measure lateral movement which basically shows how well the vehicle handles. In my case I completed the test without knocking over any cones with the hot rod pulling 0.64G which is in the high range, showing how well the car handles. I have not had the opportunity to compete at the drags, but I did have a run on the street with a Mach I Mustang 351C and managed to keep the nose of the hot rod in front.

Since the first edition of Flathead Fever was published some changes have been made to the race engine with a view to going even faster on the salt lakes.

Starting from the bottom of the engine; the oil pump is the best available without going to a dry sump, and not having an oil problem I see no point in changing it. A crank scraper is probably a good idea, but with that chunky girdle in place there is not much room for one. Upon examining the girdle I found evidence that the crank is flexing with chaffing between the centre main cap and brace, but I will have to live with that as there is not much option with a three main bearing crank.

The aluminum con rods are fine and being so light are good for a few extra horsepower over heavier steel ones (and are half the price), but being so chunky I had to relieve three of them to provide clearance for the cam.

The cam/lifter/valve combination also works well and while it has a lobe centre of 108° Crower now offer one with 111° which would lift the horsepower available higher in the rev range and given the option when purchasing I would have chosen the latter.

Some engine builders looking for more lift have line bored the cam tunnel and fitted small block Chevy cam bearings so they can increase the base circle of the cam. In my application the cam lobe is the same diameter as the bearing journal so no more lift is available and if it were more, interference with the con rods would result.

The piston/ring combination is good. The cylinder heads flow quite well after my modifications and given the option I would have preferred the one piece units which do not suffer from water leakage as experienced with the two piece ones.

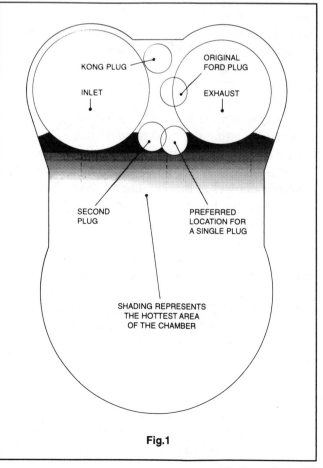

Fig.1

However the one thing I have been paying close attention to is the spark plug location. When Ford designed these engines they wanted an engine that would start easily, be reasonably economical and perform well on a marginal 4.5 volt ignition. I do not think any cylinder head designed for performance for this engine has had the plug in the right location (See fig. 1.) and have therefore decided to add a second plug per cylinder head and fire simultaneously. Having such a long chamber I believe the plug should be more central to burn the mixture more fully.

Using two plugs per cylinder is not a new idea, and in all examples that have come to my attention the second plug has been fitted directly above the piston which may be more beneficial when using methanol as opposed to gasoline as it is a much slower burning fuel requiring more timing advance.

I am also using one distributor, as opposed to others who are using two, by modifying the Mallory distributor to accept eight magnetic sensors (Hall effect) and a modified rotor. The distributor cap is discarded in favour of a dust cover while the sensors are connected to a control box and in turn eight Motor Factory brand Harley Davidson electronic coils to fire the sixteen spark plugs.

The fuel injection works well.It is easily tuneable, the engine idles more smoothly than with the Holley carb and is more responsive.It makes only five additional flywheel horsepower, but there is a big increase in torque. Unfortunately a chassis dyno is unable to accurately measure torque.

I then installed a smaller pulley on the supercharger changing the ratio from double engine speed to 2.2 over engine speed increasing the boost from 9 to 10 lb which netted an additional five horsepower at the flywheel. I have also been concerned that the supercharger, although making good horsepower is a little small so I have exchanged it for a B&M 174 cubic inch unit. These are available from Motor City Flathead who have altered the pattern of their manifold to accept the longer unit which will be driven by a ten rib belt in favour of the six rib as I have experienced some belt slip in the past. This will hopefully provide twelve pounds of boost at double engine speed.

As the supercharger is being driven up to 11,200 RPM the air/fuel mixture becomes excessively hot, so I am working on an intercooler, which is basically an aluminium radiator fitted between the supercharger and intake manifold into which is fed carbon dioxide. As CO_2 has a similar consistency to nitrous oxide, but approximately 1/3 the price, I can use a N2O bottle, line and solenoid for a total loss system.

I have made back to back tests between the engine and chassis dynos to determine the power loss through the drive train of the race car prior to any further modifications. It must be stated that the figures recorded are only accurate with this engine on the two dynos used with the power loss being 38.5%.

Having this figure available I am now collecting parts for my next race engine which will be a 284 cu. in. naturally aspirated unit. I will be using a 99 series block which is the same as my last two engines. They may not be as thick as some of the later blocks but are not as susceptible to cracking either. Other internal components to be used will include a 4-1/8" crank with steel caps, Howards aluminium con rods and probably one of the best fat tappet cams ever designed for these engines, a Potvin 425 eliminator with .412" lift and 280° duration ground on a new billet. Arias forged pistons with a 3-5/16" top radius making them pop out of the block 7/16" with .927" pins will also be fitted (refer fig. 2).

Valve train components will consist of NOS Ford lifters, overlength Manley race flow 1.72" and 1.5" valves and Isky dual springs. The block will be topped by Kong .525" heads modified as per the blown engine.

I will initially use the dual quad setup, but am experimenting with multi point fuel injection on my single quad intake.

This engine will be used in my race car to set a couple of records in the unblown classes.

The new race engine will initially use dual quad carburetors but I am also experimenting with multi-point fuel injection on my own design intake as shown above.

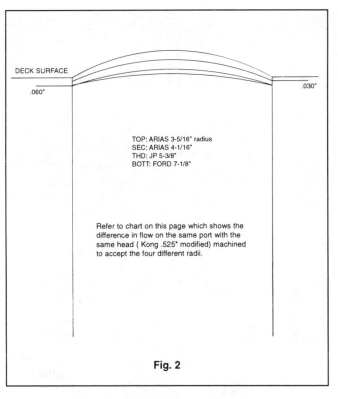

DECK SURFACE

.060" .030"

TOP: ARIAS 3-5/16" radius
SEC: ARIAS 4-1/16"
THD: JP 5-3/8"
BOTT: FORD 7-1/8"

Refer to chart on this page which shows the
difference in flow on the same port with the
same head (Kong .525" modified) machined
to accept the four different radii.

Fig. 2

Lift	075	150	225	300	375	450
Dome	CFM					
7-1/8" R	27.4	40.4	48.7	54.6	58.3	60.9
5-3/8" R	27.2	40.7	49.0	55.0	58.8	60.9
4-1/16" R	27.0	40.7	48.6	55.0	58.8	60.9
3-5/16" R	26.8	41.6	50.4	57.1	60.9	63.4

The second test shows quite an improvement with the block relieved to a depth of .100"

Lift	075	150	225	300	375	450
Dome	CFM					
7-1/8" R	27.4	43.3	55.0	64.5	71.4	76.1
5-3/8" R	27.2	42.7	53.7	63.0	69.3	74.5
4-1/16" R	27.2	41.9	51.6	60.4	67.2	72.4
3-5/16" R	26.2	41.0	51.6	60.4	67.7	73.0

The third test shows continued improvement with the block relieved to a depth of .200"

Lift	075	150	225	300	375	450
Dome	CFM					
7-1/8" R	29.4	46.6	60.0	71.4	79.2	85.0
5-3/8" R	29.4	47.2	60.9	71.9	79.8	85.5
4-1/16" R	29.4	47.2	60.9	71.9	79.8	85.0
3-5/16" R	29.0	47.2	60.9	71.9	79.9	85.5

The old saying "There is more than one way to skin a cat" holds true with Ford engines. Flatheads were fitted with flat top pistons until 1937, and some engine builders are currently building their engines using them in conjunction with extensively modified combustion chambers to give quite good flow. However there is a trade off in compression ratios in keeping with the manufacturers original specifications making them more suitable for a supercharged application.

I have drawn this cross sectional view to show the advantage of using "pop up" pistons in a naturally aspired engine to increase compression without sacrificing airflow. I have machined a Kong .525" cylinder head with four different radii, and with four matching pistons, installed them in a factory relieved (.100" deep) block and CC'd them with the following results:

7-1/8" R – 7.62:1
5-3/8" R – 8.02:1
4-1/16" R – 8.33:1
3-5/16" R – 9.57:1

I then installed the test block on the flow bench and checked the four combustion chambers on the same port. I carried out this test three times, the first with no valve relief and as would be expected quite poor results:

CONCLUSION

Increasing the dome of the piston will give more compression and has little or no effect on flow. The deeper the relief, the greater the flow, but the lower the compression, telling us something we already know, the shape of the port/combustion chamber is more important than size.

MANIFOLDING

While recently dyno testing a customer's engine I did a back to back test with my modified single quad top (page 57) and a 6101 single quad top (developed for marine use). The horsepower figures were the same, but the 6101 was down 5 ft lb of torque which was picked up after modifying as per the dotted line.

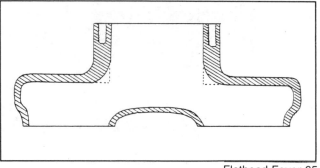

A FLATHEAD FOR THE STREET

The bulk of this book is based on information derived from the author's two engines, one for all out race use and the other for dual purpose street and strip applications. There is no doubt that both engines are stout performers, but what if you don't want to go quite that far with your own street version? You will obviously glean plenty of information from the rest of this book that will be a great help to you in building a more sedate street engine, but this chapter is purely to illustrate that you can build a pure street version of the flathead that performs well but won't cost you the earth.

The photos accompanying this chapter are of Wayne Ryan's project car, a superb 1932 Ford tudor street rod powered by a '53 flathead that has been worked just enough for spritely street performance and suitably dressed as only a flathead can be.

The block has been bored 0.40" to give a final displacement of 244 cubic inches. The crankshaft, rods and pistons are all stock type items, but the spinning internal components have been balanced. Standard rings and bearings are used but the flywheel has been lightened by 9lb. A high volume oil pump is fitted along with a mild grind Camshaft that features 275° duration and .320" lift. The inlet valves open at 27° and close at 68° while the exhausts open at 65° and close at 29°. Johnson adjustable lifters are used to operate standard valves.

Feeding the flathead is an Offenhauser inlet manifold mounting triple Stromberg 97 carbies, the rodders favourite over the years. Early Offenhauser finned heads raise the compression and add to the appearance of the engine and a Mallory twin point distributor fires the mixture. Elsewhere in this book you will read of the modifications necessary to fit the early style heads with centre coolant outlets to the later flathead block. An owner made stainless

steel exhaust system takes away the spent gases.

Backing up the engine is a Ford Toploader gearbox coupled to the engine using an original pressure plate and Falcon 6 cylinder clutch. The shifter is a Hurst item. Note that the tudor also sports an air conditioner so the Ryan family can enjoy all the modern comforts but without sacrificing the pure nostalgia of a flathead engine.

Wayne's engine was built by the author of this book.

ABOUT THE AUTHOR

Mike Davidson has been a hot rodder for more than twenty years and he has always been a keen flathead fan. His first street rod was a '32 Ford roadster which naturally was flathead powered. In its final form it sported a B&M 144 blower on a modified original flathead manifold, before B&M had released a complete kit to facilitate this arrangement.

The engine was a '39 model bored to 244 cubic inches and fed by a 465 Holley on top of the blower which was 40% overdriven. This package was later updated to a 1/8 x 1/8 engine of 268 cubic inches with Isky Max 1 camshaft, Offenhauser heads and the blower overdrive stepped up to 65%. It also featured Isky single valve springs, Belond headers and JP pistons along with a modified crab style distributor.

Stage two of Mike's flathead development work saw him produce his first pure race engine. This engine was a 281 cubic inch version with an Isky 410 Accelerator cam, dual Isky valve springs, JP pistons, Offenhauser cylinder heads, a Weiand

Below: Mike Davidson's first street rod was this '32 Ford roadster which was of course flathead powered.

The engine in the '32 roadster featured a B&M blower mounted on a modified original manifold, before B&M released a kit to make this swap easy.

intake modified to take two Holley 450 Economaster carbs and a Mallory dual point distributor. This combination was the first powertrain to be used in his salt lake racer and it recorded a speed of 129 m.p.h. on Lake Gairdner in South Australia, Mike's home state.

This in turn led to the ultimate powerplant now residing in Mike's race car and which is also described in full detail throughout this book in which it is referred to as the "Race Engine". It was this ultimate engine which powered the salt lake racer to 162 m.p.h. on Lake Gairdner in March

Above: The milder street/race version of the flathead powers Mike's latest street rod, a '22 T roadster that will be used essentially for street use with an occasional outing at the drags. This is the engine that is referred to throughout this book as the "Street Engine".

Below: The first pure race engine was a 281 cubic inch version with Weiand intake modified to take two Holley 450 Economaster carbs and a Mallory dual point distributor.

Above and at left is the full-on race engine that powered Mike's salt lake racing roadster to over 160 m.p.h. on Lake Gairdner in March 1995 and which is referred to throughout this book as the "Race Engine". Flathead engines don't get much wilder than this one!

1995 despite spinning out twice due to windy conditions. Mike is yet to use the nitrous oxide injection on this engine for a full power run and he will increase the blower overdrive ratio for more boost and potentially even greater speed. A bellypan will be added to the car to help streamline the underside and reduce turbulence. His long term aim is to rebody the salt lake racer with a stretched Fiat Topolino body to put the car into vintage competition coupe class and hopefully over the 200 m.p.h. mark.

A FLATHEAD ALBUM

The Auburn Auto Machine bellytank lakester uses an injected flathead engine to chase records on the Bonneville salt flats.

The Weir/Rea/Mumford team put together this tidy '23 T roadster for salt lake racing on Lake Gairdner. It has been developed and updated from a very basic, mildly worked flathead to the point where it now runs a 256 cubic inch version with Kong heads and Hilborn fuel injection. Top speed so far is close to 120 m.p.h.

Surrey Street Rodders built their bellytank lakester in England and transported it to Bonneville in 1992 to test the flathead power-plant only to miss out because of a rained out meet. The engine is a 256 cubic inch version with GMC blower that is backed by a ZF four speed gearbox and Halibrand quickchange rear end. Drivers are Paul Wright and Viv Bowyer, crew members are Kevin Monks, Nick Martin and Geoff Mitchell.

Above: Swap meets are a good place to search for flathead speed equipment. This collection of intake manifolds was spotted at the N.S.R.A. Street Rod Nationals in Louisville, Kentucky.

Below: The beautiful bodywork on the Kelly and Hall '34 Ford roadster salt lake racer hides a Hilborn injected 281 cubic inch flathead engine.

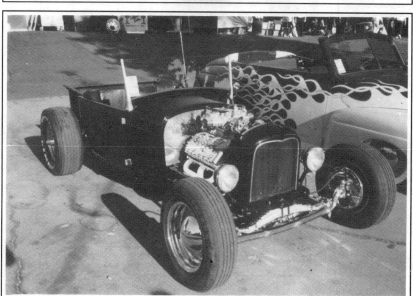

Nothing quite measures up to a flathead in a street rod for pure nostalgia. This group of photos illustrates several variations on the street flathead theme but all give the impression of fun times with the old hot rodders favourite, the flathead Ford V8 engine.

FLATHEAD SUPPLIERS DIRECTORY

Mike's Sidevalve Supply.
12 Nottage Tce., Medindie Gardens, S.A. 5081
Australia. 61 8 344 8561

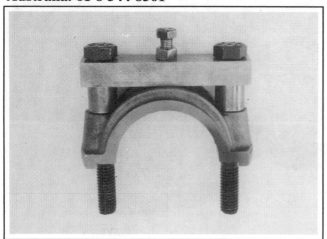

Main bearing support.

Exhaust port dividers.

Intake manifold.

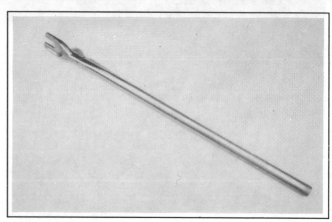

Valve lifting bar.

Distributor spacer and drive.

C4 and Powerglide bellhousing.

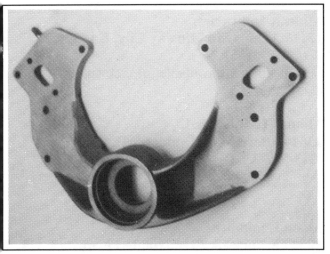

Saddle mount.

Early alternator bracket. Late alternator bracket.

Anderson's Race & Restoration.
3027 Jefferson St., San Diego, CA. 92110.
(619-295-1106)
New and used parts and services.

Antique Auto Parts.
9113 East Garvey Ave., Rosemond, CA. 91770.
(818-288-2121)
Large selection of new engine and chassis parts
and accessories.

Automatic Transmission Specialties.
2195 Commercial St. NE, Salem, OR. 97303.
(503-364-6194)
Flatomatic C4 to flathead adapter kit.

Baron Racing Equipment.
19051 Blythe St., Reseda, CA. 91335.
(818-718-8451)
Intake manifold suit 4 webers or injection and
cylinder heads, main caps & girdles.

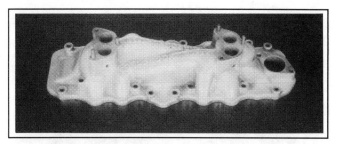

Edelbrock Corp.
2700 California St., Torrance, CA. 90503.
(310-781-2222)
Cylinder heads and super dual intake.

Flathead Jack.
P.O. Box 31175, Walnut Creek, CA. 94598.
(510-932-2233)
Range of engine parts.

Flatout Racing Products.
39660 86th St., West Leona Valley, CA .
(805-270-0141)
Performance, modifications & services.

Fuel Injection Engineering.
26641 Cabot Road, Laguna Hills, CA. 92653
(714-582-1170)
Hilborn fuel injection.

Hot Rod & Custom Supply.
1304 SE 10th St., Cape Coral, FL. 33990.
(813-574-7744)
Full range of engine parts, access. and services.

Iskenderian Cams.
16020 S Broadway, Gardena, CA. 90248.
(213-770-0930)
Selection of camshafts.

Doug King.
2400 Stanton Hill Rd., Castro Valley, CA.
94546.
(510-537-3909)
Main caps and girdles.

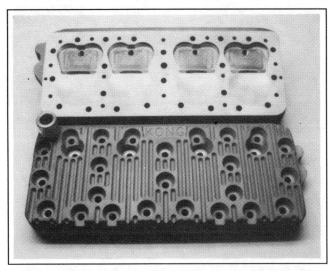

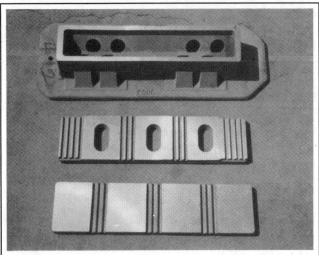

Kong Engineering.
4629 Alger St., Los Angeles, CA. 90039.
(818-247-3968)
Cylinder heads and intake manifolds suit 2, 3, 4
carbs or supercharger.

Mallory Ignition Products.
550 Mallory Way, Carson City, NV. 89701.
(702-882-6600)
Dual point, Unilite and Magnetic Breakerless distributors to suit all flatheads.

Midway Industries.
15116 Adams St., Midway City, CA. 92655.
(714-373-6155)
Stinger ignitions available for crab and 8BA type
distributors.

Motor City Flathead.
13624 Stawell Rd., Dundee, MI. 48131
(313-529-3363)
Full range of engine parts, accessories and services.

Moon Equipment.
10820 S Norwalk Blvd., Sante Fe Springs, CA.
90670.
(310-946-2961)
Selection of camshafts.

Navaro Engineering.
4212 Chevy Chase Dve., Los Angeles, CA.
90039.
(818-241-6644)
Cylinder heads and intake mainfolds.

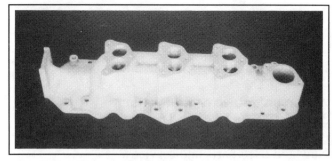

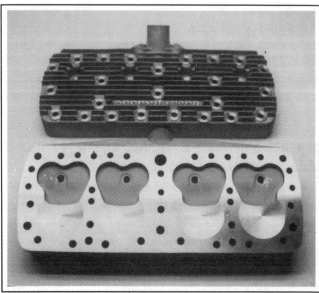

Offenhauser Sales Corp.
5232 Alhambra Ave., Los Angeles, CA. 90032.
(213-225-1307)
Full range of cylinder heads intake manifolds link-
ages, adaptors, bellhousings.

Patrick's Antique.
80 Box 10648, Casa Grande, AZ. 85230.
(602-836-1117)
Full range of engine parts and accessories.

Red's Headers.
5832 Gibbons, Carmichael, CA. 95608.
(916-488-4532)
Selection of headers.

Roto-Faze Ignitions.
23136 Mariposa Ave., Torrance, CA. 90502.
(310-325-8844)
Performance ignitions for late flatheads.

Schneider Racing Cams.
1235 Cushman Ave., San Diego, CA. 92110.
(619-297-0227)
Large selection of camshafts.

Joe Smith Ford & Street Rod Parts
3070 Briarcliff Rd. NE, Atlanta GA. 30329
(404-634-5157)
Range of engine parts.

Speedway Motors.
300 Van Dorn, Lincoln, NE. 68501-1906.
(402-474-4411)
Full range of engine parts and accessories.

Ted's Auto Parts.
2561 Woods Blvd., Lincoln, NE 68502.
(402-560-4470)
New and used parts.

Vern Tardel.
464 Pleasant Ave., Santa Rosa, CA. 95401.
(707-838-6065)
Range of services.

Weber Cams.
1663 Superior Ave., Costa Mesa, CA. 92627.
Large selection of camshafts.

INDEX